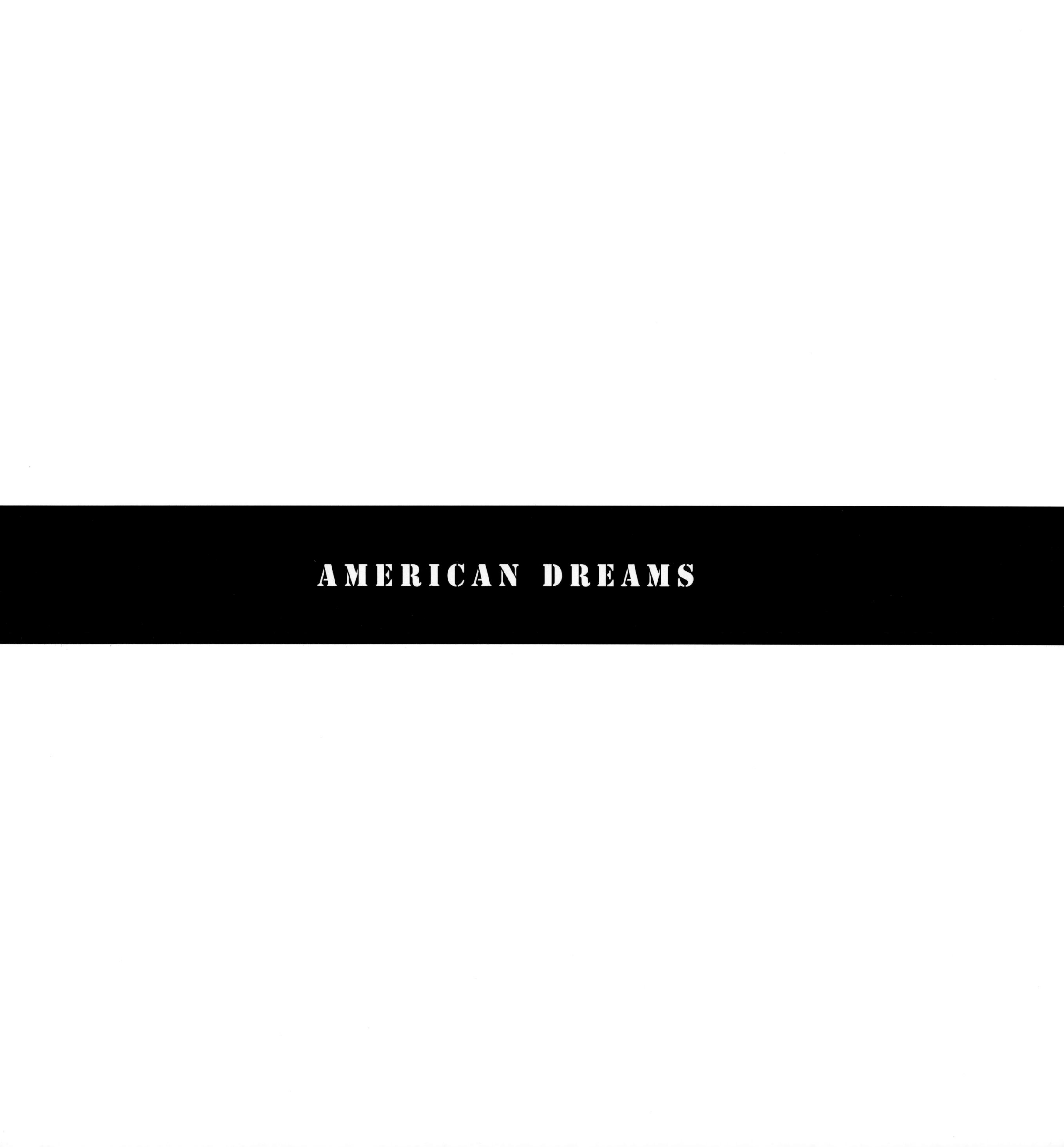
AMERICAN DREAMS

Statue of Liberty, New York City, **1996**

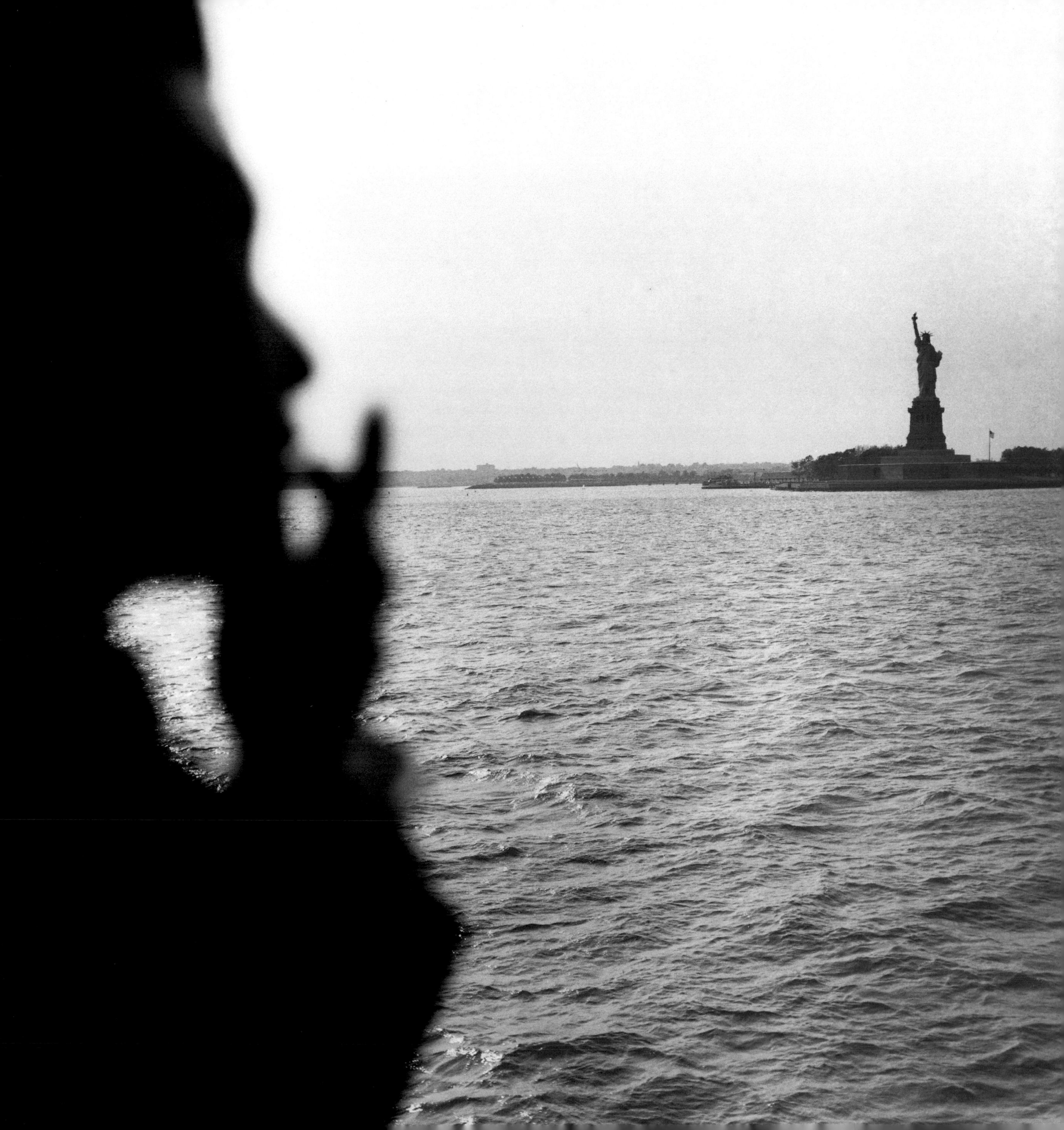

Christmas parade, Huntsville, Texas, **1995**

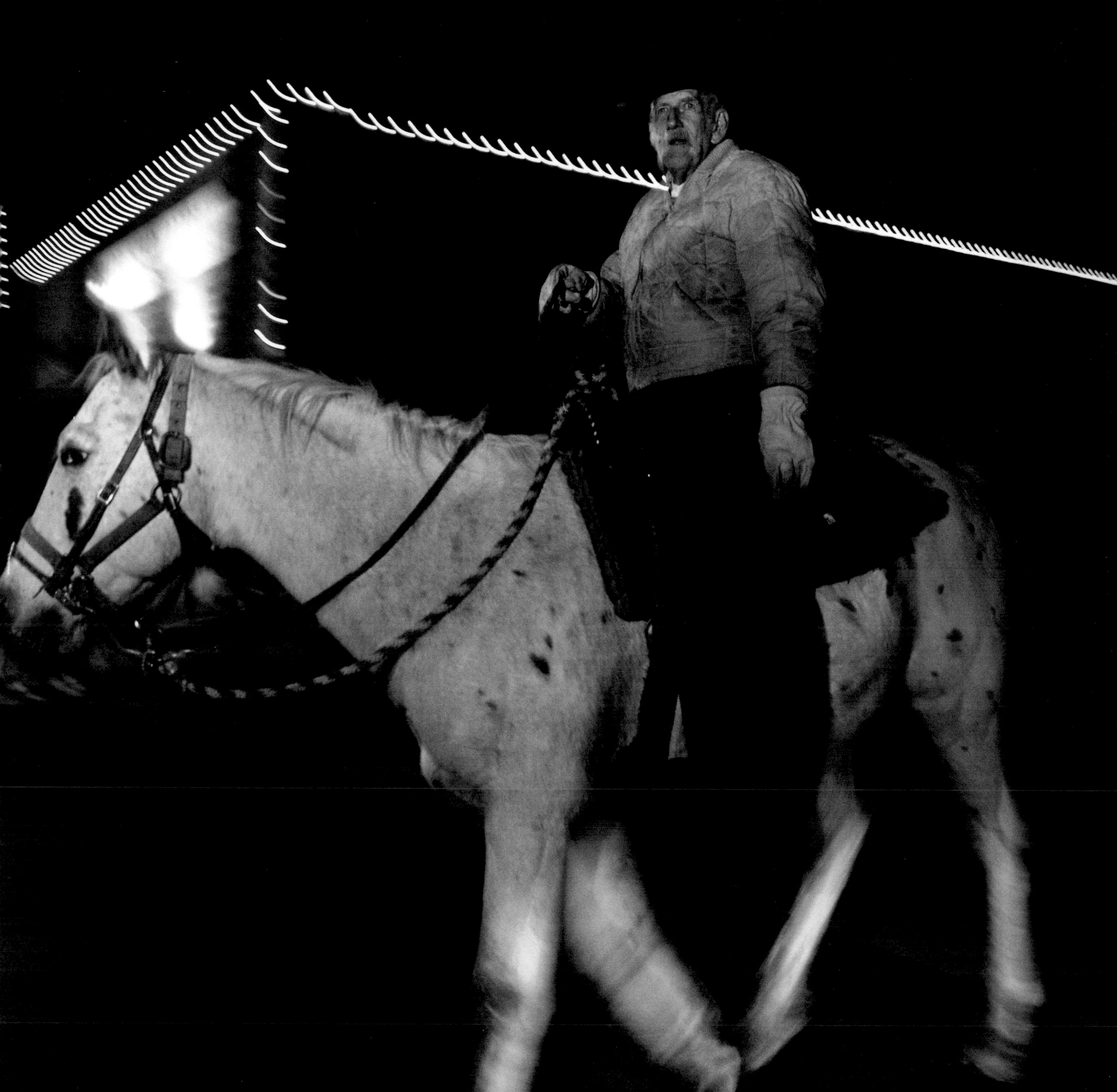

College student on the beach at Daytona Beach, Florida, **1995**

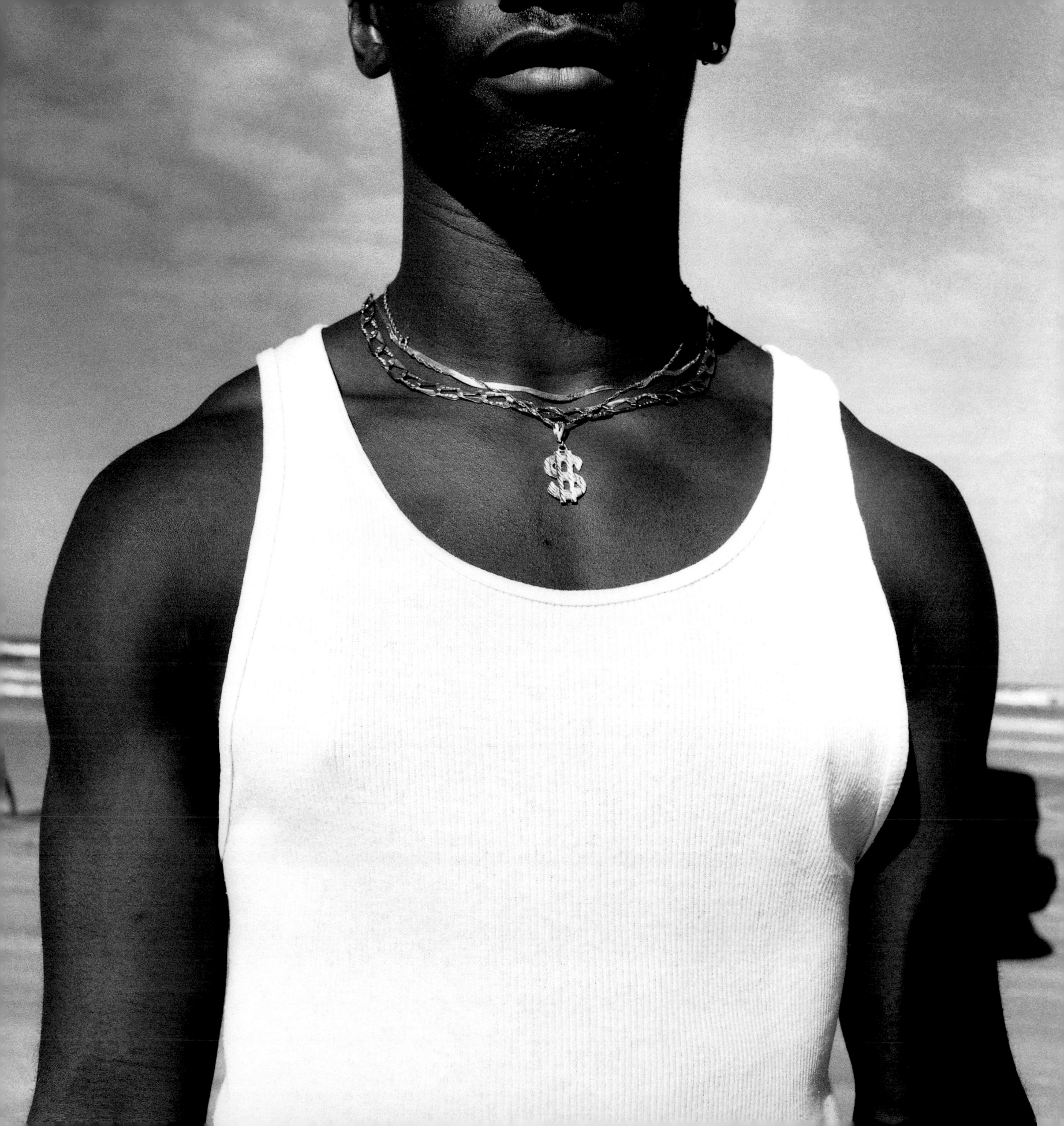

Cheerleaders in the Thanksgiving Day parade, New York City, **1996**

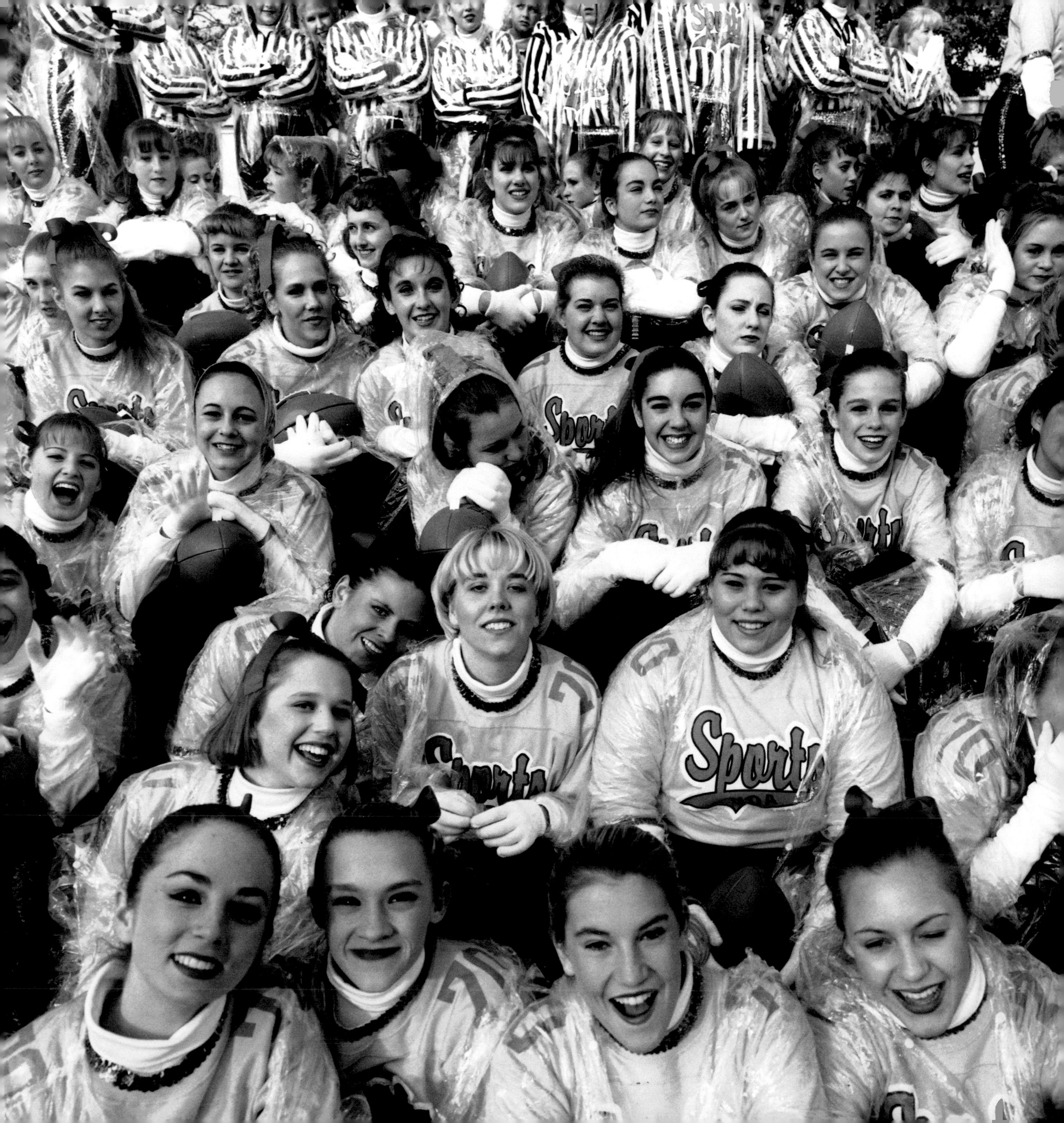
Sports

View of Midtown Manhattan
from the UN building, New York City, **1996**

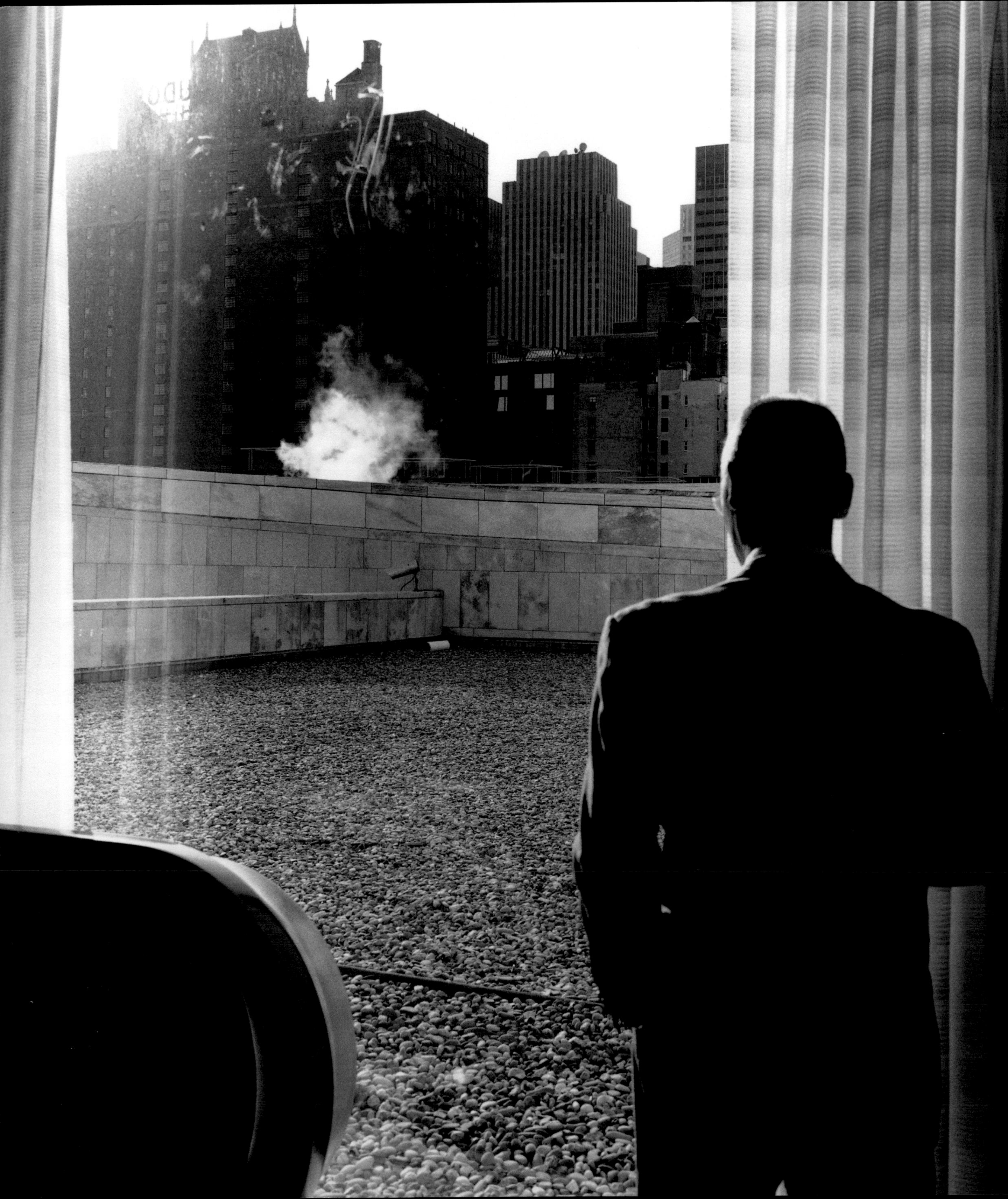

BASTIENNE SCHMIDT

AMERICAN DREAMS

Edited by Hans-Georg Pospischil
Texts by Vicki Goldberg and Bastienne Schmidt

EDITION STEMMLE

For my mother

CONTENTS

AMERICAN DREAMS

Bastienne Schmidt:
Slightly Tattered Dreams

Vicki Goldberg

The Puritans thought that God had intended to shed his grace on America: in fact, most thought the Lord had already delivered it with a warranty. Long before we were a nation, the new land was referred to as A City on a Hill, a shining city to be watched by all, not a utopia but a place where a society could be constructed on a plan and humanity could stand a little nearer to the angels. No one ever thought it was perfection here, but most harbored the expectation that we might come closer than usual. And though we have never had a lack of critics and have probably been the most self-analytical and self critical nation in the world, taken all in all we thought for a couple of centuries that the promise had been properly held out to us. In this century the Depression put a crimp in that belief, but victory in World War II brought it roaring back.

And then success sent us reeling. Beats and intellectuals set out on the road in search of America, and if they loved what they found they hated it too, and railed against consumerism and conformity. In the sixties, students picked up this message and ran with it, while the civil rights struggle and the Vietnam war spread disillusion far beyond the gates of the universities. It wasn't just that the image of America was changing in people's minds. It was changing on paper and in the media too. It had become possible to look at the nation from another vantage point, where the promises looked a little ragged around the edges.

Among photographers the telling event was the publication of Robert Frank's *The Americans* in 1959. (It was first published in France the previous year.) In the best tradition of the 1930s Frank had gone on the road in search of America, but the only city he saw on the hill was dispirited and more than a little bleak. His abrupt, off-kilter style was unfamiliar, and his odd and lively affection for the loneliness, the mass-produced trash and fast-food joints he spied on his journeys was not always so evident and at any rate hard to fathom. But what struck observers hardest and upset them most was Frank's sense of the sad, tough and tired heart of America the beautiful.

Frank actually made visible a cultural shift, a self image in the process of transformation, that was already in the works, but he gave it such definitive visual form that his influence is still being felt. Bastienne Schmidt takes a cue from *The Americans*; her book is a kind of off-beat commentary on that classically off-beat document. She is clearly in tune with Frank's spirit of brash and skeptical inquiry and his willingness to look directly at the people, the places and moments that will never win trophies in a competitive land. Often she comes in uncomfortably close, cropping the subject bluntly. Other times she views the world at an angle or catches it, hazily defined, on the wing. In short she keeps her Rolleiflex, a medium-format camera, within the precincts of Frank's influence on 35mm street photography.

Schmidt is more confrontational than Frank; her subjects often see her coming and regard her without fear. In byways and gathering places and quiet corners she fastens onto a detail, a look, a gesture that speaks in a scene that would otherwise be mute. Curious about the occasions that bring crowds together, she sees America as a country in such constant motion that the still camera cannot keep up with it.

Hers is not everyone's America but an album of what few tourists and fewer residents have noticed, a land that takes both entertainment and death seriously, where singers smile without cease and watchers of every sort, even camera watchers, stare fixedly. This America, mourning some of its tattered dreams, is intent on having a good time but not altogether up to the task.

Both Schmidt and Frank were foreign born – she grew up in Germany and Greece – giving them the kind of outsider's perspective that an astute observer would take advantage of. Frank came from an atmosphere of post-war European anti-Americanism, but Schmidt says she was looking for something more tantalizing, the myth she knew from TV and American exports. Partly because Frank's images marked a change in the cultural weather, her view of grave young souls, cross-eyed cowboys and ruffled-shirted ballyhoo artists won't provoke outrage, but her book too records a sharp-eyed foreigner's glance at surprises, incongruities, disappointments, and a few sweet moments in ill-fitting jackets. Most tellingly, Schmidt has a sharp sense of the times: she brings us smack up against her vision of the 1990s, when America, comprehensible or not, can only be considered in the light of the changes that have recently overtaken it.

Is it possible to picture a cheery America after Robert Frank? Well, that rather depends on who your audience is. Ronald Reagan insisted it was morning in America all the time. *Time* magazine as recently as July of 1997 had a cover story called "The Backbone of America" that mentioned some of the down side but kept the pictures pleasant. Most serious readers won't accept unmitigated good cheer after the civil rights struggles of the 1960s, the Vietnam War, assassinations, Watergate and subsequent revelations. Some consider us a nation that has gained the whole world and lost its soul. Serious photography watchers would probably be taken aback by a vision of happiness spreading coast to coast. Perhaps by now we look at our country as if we were foreigners too.

Both *The Americans* and *American Dreams* are road books, records of that great American place, the road, and documents of twentieth century survey expeditions. Nineteenth century expeditions brought back images of uncharted lands as a prelude to development; today photographers go in search of social and psychic discoveries. Walker Evans's *American Photographs* of 1938, which strongly influenced Robert Frank, is the *locus classicus* for this kind of visual diary, but the road has also drawn writers and reporters from Jack Kerouac to John Steinbeck to Charles Kuralt. Frank memorialized the road in its endlessness, isolation and invitation to fatigue, and Schmidt in her way does too, sometimes catching the mindless, half melancholy looks of passengers watching the land roll by.

She repeatedly invokes the American flag, which for Frank was an organizing device. He saw it worn thin on July 4 or blotting out the faces of its followers. She sees it on a clothes line on July 4 or blown by the wind to hide three men in suits: their legs hold up the emblem of the nation, but only one leg of the central figure is visible, as if the country's support were unsteady, off, irregular at its center.

Both photographers are unusually alert to the signs of death. Frank went to a black funeral, so did she. He looked at car accidents, grave markers, cemeteries; she looks at mourners and commemorations. Her photographs suggest that she has a highly developed sense of sorrow. (Schmidt's first book, *Vivir la Muerte*, was a moving study of the rituals of death in Latin America, where the end of life is more closely integrated into the living culture than it is in either Europe or North America. That book was Schmidt's attempt to come to terms with her own father's death – the mourning process as a photographic quest for understanding.) Frank presented the simple facts, as bare and stark as a grave marker or a mourner at a moment of sadness and perplexity. Schmidt looks at mourners too in all their grief, but she focusses on the changes that have overtaken the nature of death and our response to it under the pressures of recent history.

The signal event that opened the gates of disillusion and distrust in this country was a death: the assassination of President John F. Kennedy on November 22, 1963. Schmidt takes pictures of mourners visiting his grave three decades later and photographing it to prove they have been there. She also snaps his brother Robert's grave, another index of assassination, and a more recent monument, a mural of Selena, the beloved Mexican-born singer who was murdered by a disgruntled employee in 1995. Assassination and murder as signposts on which to string the history of a country ...

There is one astonishing picture of commemoration here: a wax museum display of Jackie Kennedy, veiled, and her two young children about to march in JFK's funeral procession, a three-dimensional rendering of a photograph. The American flag hangs down beside the figures, in case we missed the significance. Every American who was alive at the time has a photographic image of these three at that very moment indelibly burned into the brain. Jackie and her children were on

TV for what seemed like hours that day, and the black-and-white photographs of them have never entirely dropped from view. They fixed the national sense of grief and gave viewers someone to focus on and identify with, while Jackie Kennedy's sorrow, stoicism and immense dignity raised her to heroic stature across the land. In the wax museum, improbably, she *smiles*. Death, which comes even to Presidents, need not be too disturbing after all.

Though Schmidt makes no claim to document all of America and indeed says she does not even understand it, her eye lights on evidence of some of the most telling issues of our time. The memory of assassination and the potential for murder are joined by a photograph of the AIDS quilt, with the mourners in anonymous silhouette in the distance, while a framed picture of a handsome man when he was still in good enough health and smiling casts a shadow over the signatures on the quilt. Elsewhere a decorated veteran stands by the Vietnam wall: more names of the dead, lest we forget. And a black man with enormous, haunted eyes sits on death row, where so many more blacks than whites wait for execution in a country that embraces it more avidly than almost any other in the West. Even the prison's so-called Death Bed (which might more aptly be called an execution bed) sits – looms – for its portrait looking like some peculiar crucifix redundantly bound with belts.

Then there's the American preoccupation with guns, which account for too many of our death statistics. Here's a gun shop, here a gun club where the rifles are laid out across the bedspreads with loving care and orderliness, and there three tough, pretty and confident teen-age girls posing with their rifles at a shooting camp, not every parent's notion of a summer camp for girls.

The race issue that Frank traced across America Schmidt traces too, but now it has a new slant, in line with historical shifts. Black history is today a subject of wide study, black ancestry newly venerated. A woman in African garb, knee deep in the sea, performs a commemorative service for slaves who lost their lives. If this existed in the 1950s and 1960s, most white didn't know about it.

And race is no longer merely a question of black and white but of many cultures and ethnicities in a society transformed by shifts in immigration patterns and ethnic awareness. A young Latin American woman stands beneath two portraits of Elvis in a New York beauty salon. A man with the profile of a South American Indian rides a bus, or a train, across the West. An Asiatic singer greets his fans in a town made famous by country music. Schmidt's camera comes right up on the torso of a border patrol officer, bullets gleaming at his belt, as he surveys the fence built on this side to keep people on that one from crossing over. We are much more various now, and much more conscious of being so, and still rattled about how to deal with difference.

Then there's money. A young black man on spring break in Florida is cut off by the frame at nose and waist so the dollar sign on a chain about his neck lies in the center of the picture. An East Los Angeles mural is pictured at such a slant that the dollar bills floating down on one side of the painted image fly right out toward us. A Beverly Hills real estate agent in tight beige clothes works two phones at once; behind her are pictures of classical ruins that not even Hollywood agents could sell.

For all her references to Frank and his style, Schmidt's eye is all her own. She views American oddities and preoccupations with an unconventional intensity: Young children playing video games as determinedly as if they were adult gamblers. The Wigwam Motel's display of imitation tepees topped by electric lights. Gravely awkward children got up like lampshades and candy boxes for a christening. Obese older women isolated like monuments in the ocean shallows. Black boys on a jungle gym, as grimly serious as men worn down by centuries of injustice. A black woman having her hair braided in what might be a sacrificial ritual.

This being the 1990s, Schmidt plays with recurrent images of spectatorship in small towns and large. People watch parades or stare out windows at nothing in particular just because it is there. The photographer herself is a spectator, of course and we, looking at what she offers us, are the audience for a foreign production of the American follies, or perhaps of an American tragedy, or maybe America the beautiful without quite as much grace as promised. Frank showed us a Hollywood starlet ogled by envious fans, Schmidt goes to a Miss Olympia Body Building contest, where the goal of blonde and lissome has been replaced by strenuous efforts to look like Hulk Hogan in a bikini. A tourist in Monument Valley trains his camera on the sky, others tour the Valley with their lunches in plastic bags and unwrap them by the unlikely outcroppings where John Wayne used to ride. The stars and their fans bring their smiles, their guitars and patience to Branson, Missouri for big-time country music year after year.

Schmidt takes a seat in the front row of the spectacle, so close she sometimes sees fragments or comes up against complexities that crowd in when backgrounds are cut out. The performers on stage – us – are often in motion, or the world is whirling past them faster than they know in blurs and streaks of light. Minor players, wanting a chance in the limelight, thrust a hand or an arm past the edge of the frame. Occasionally Schmidt bears witness to the almost empty stage of the American landscape, occasionally catches an actor off guard, waiting, watching: sad, wary, resigned, quietly alert for whatever comes next. The drama erratically unfolding before her camera is a sober one. Emotions at high pitch (or maybe just high smolder) crop up three or four times where you might not think they belonged.

She came to the spectacle as foreigners do, on a ship passing the Statue of Liberty in the book's first picture. As the curtain comes down on her version of *American dreams* she is still looking at America, photographing herself now, this time with the Statue of Liberty behind her. And as she snaps a picture of Bastienne Schmidt with a camera to her eye, the camera facing out of the picture, she looks for all the world as if she were photographing us.

I.

Flag parade on 5th Avenue, New York City, **1987**

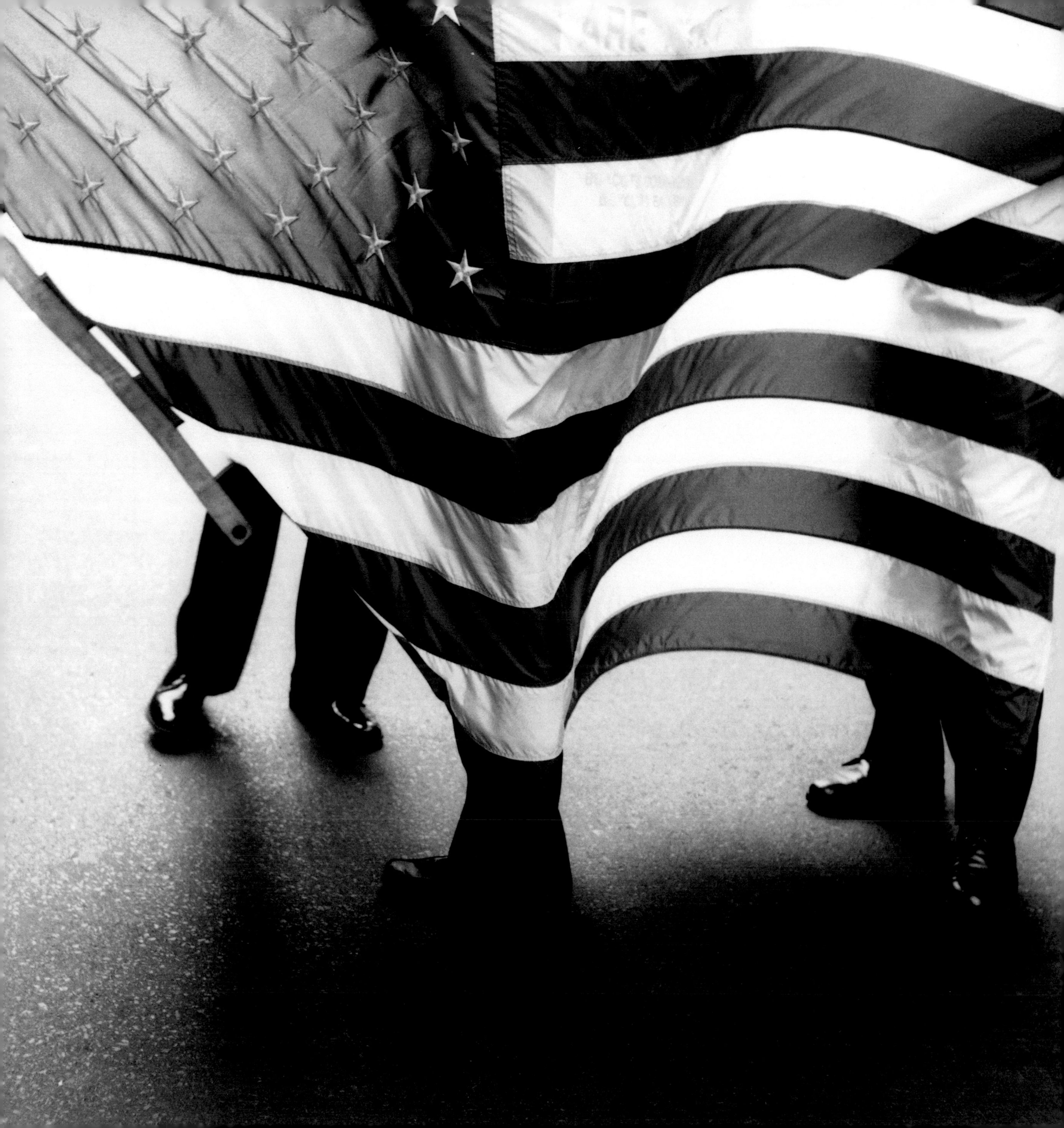

American border policeman
on a daily patrol along the US-Mexican border,
San Diego, California, **1994**

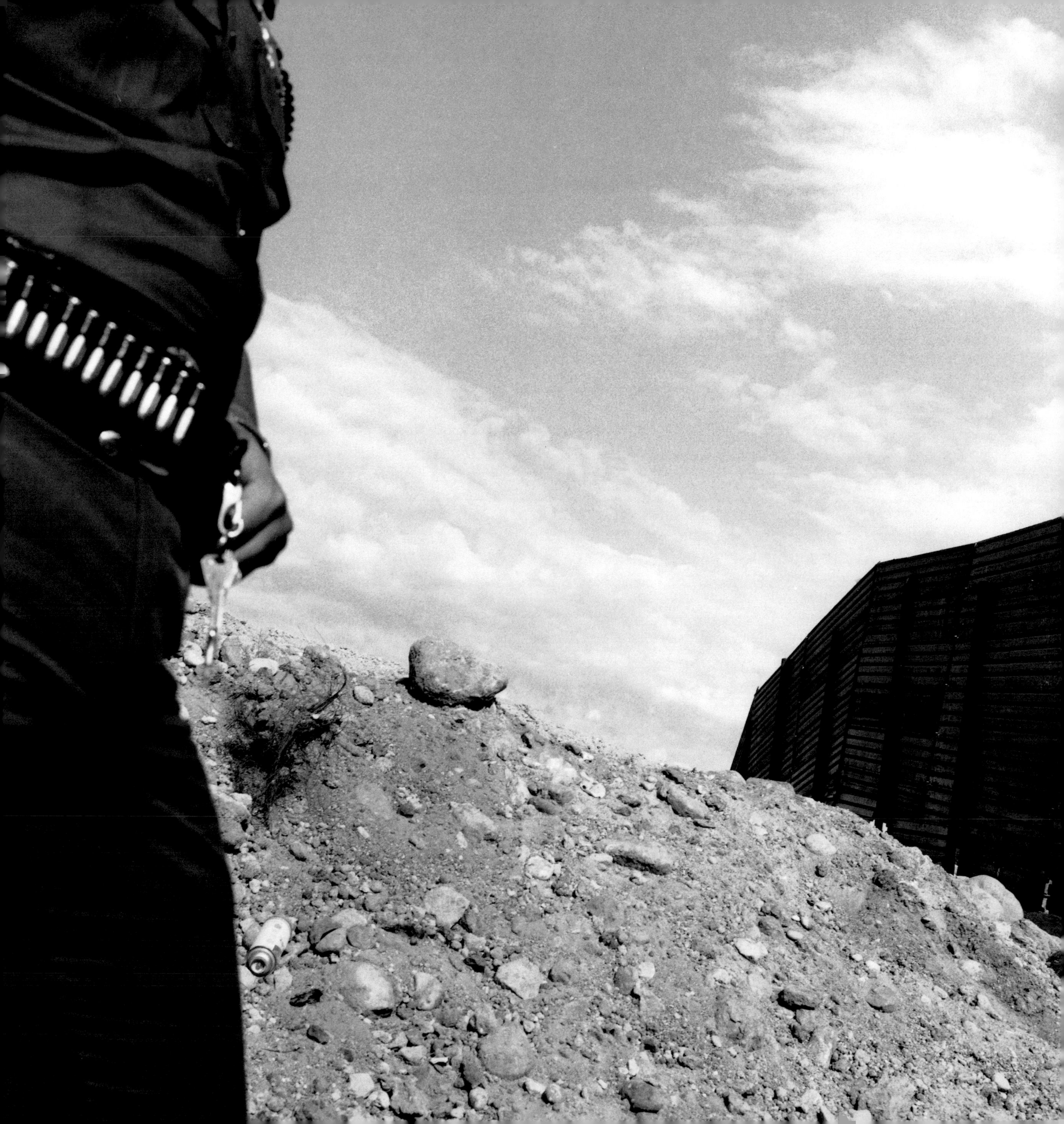

Mexican dances performed for tourists,
Olvera Street, Los Angeles, California. **1993**

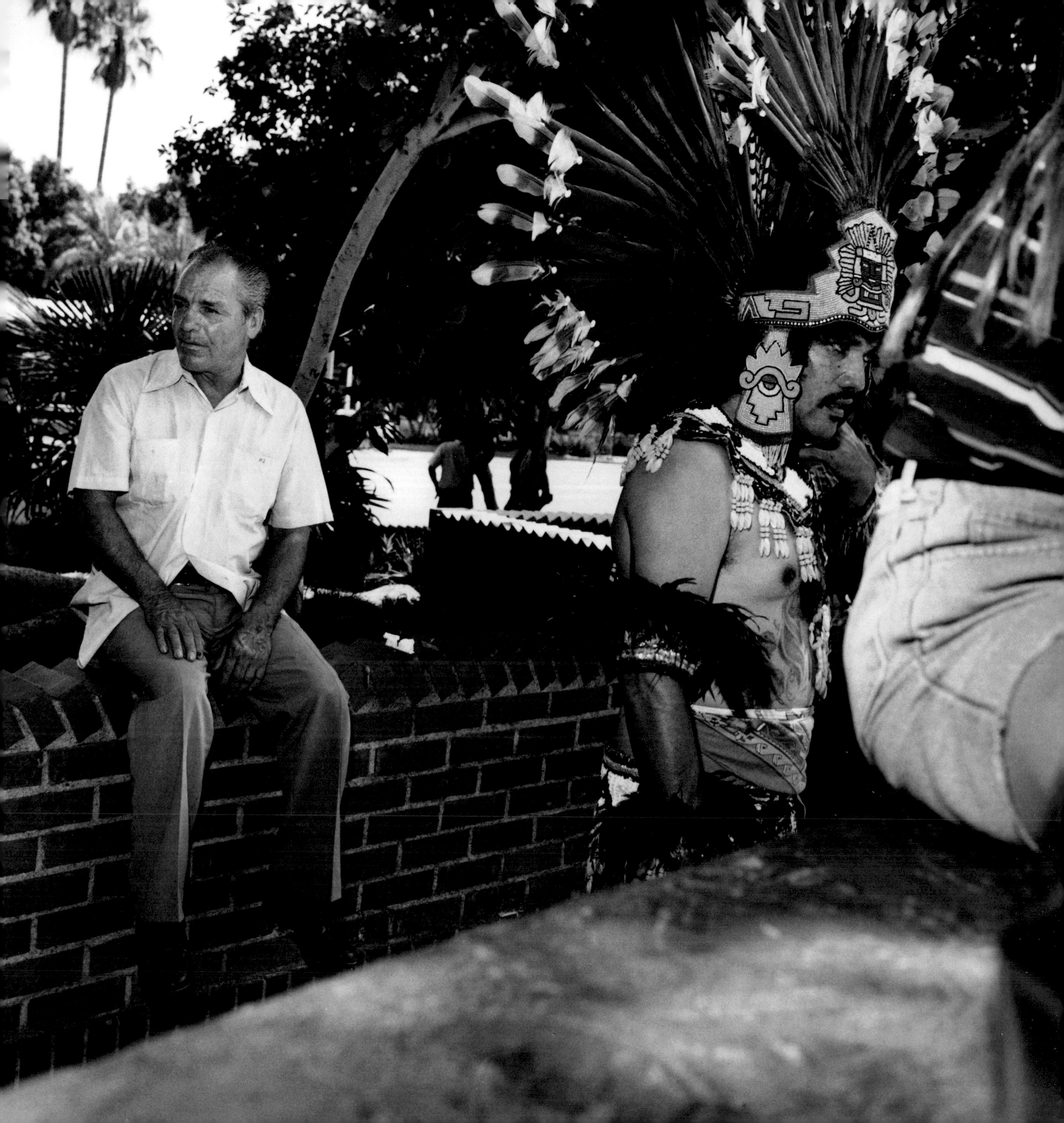

Group baptism in the Mexican La Plazita Church,
Los Angeles, California, **1993**

Families get together on the beach at Venice Beach,
California, **1993**

On the beach at Daytona Beach,
Florida, **1995**

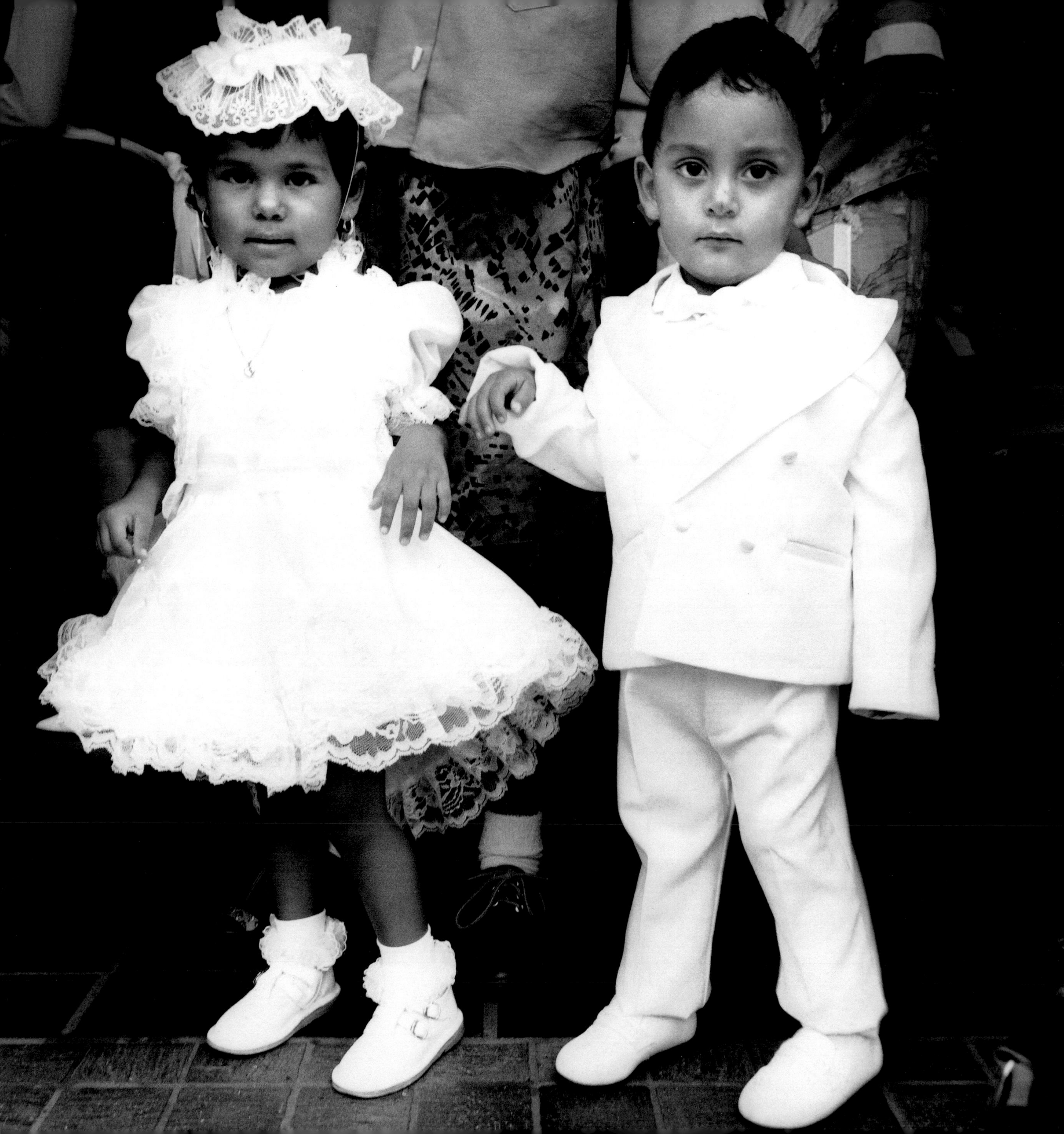

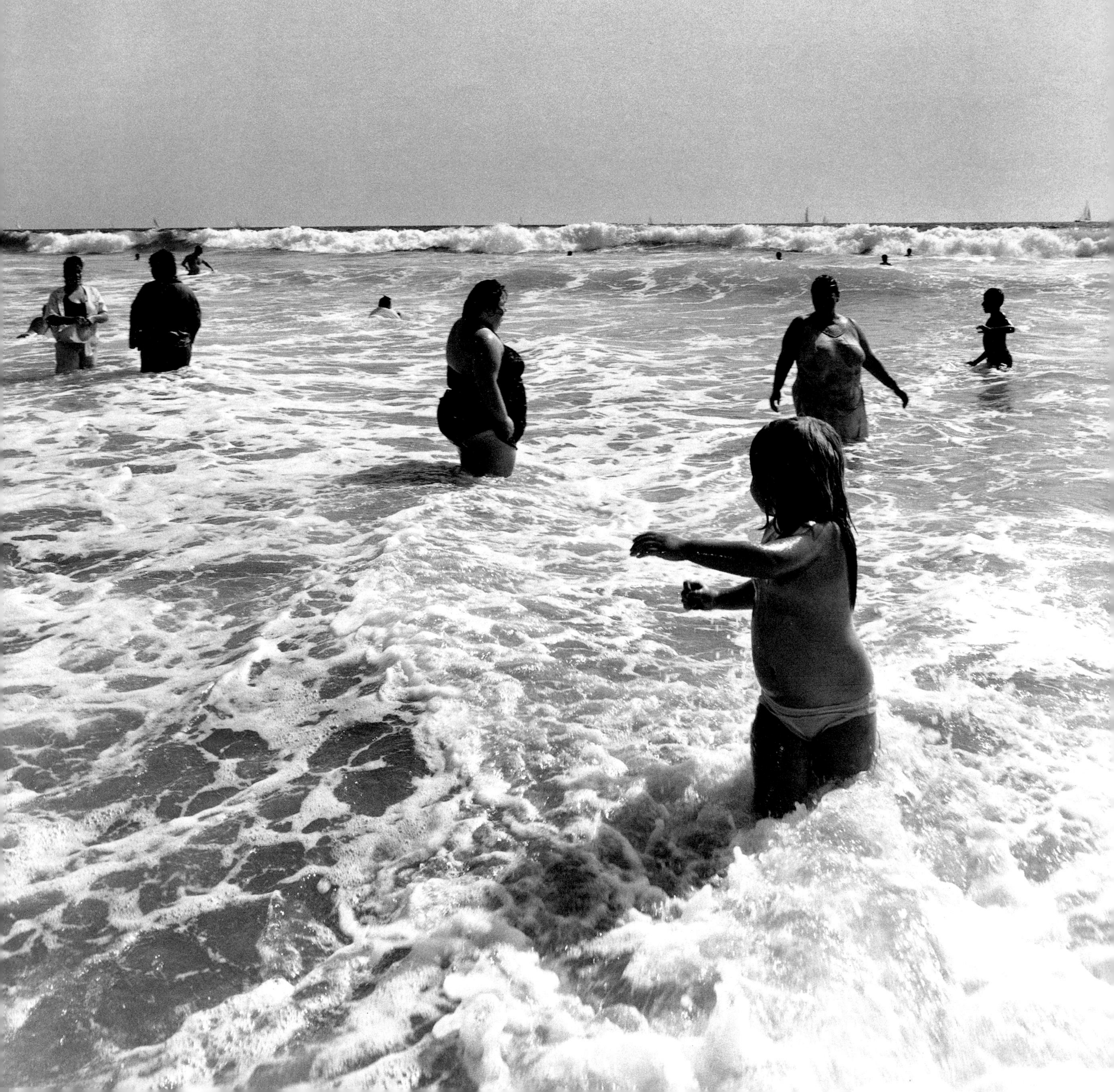

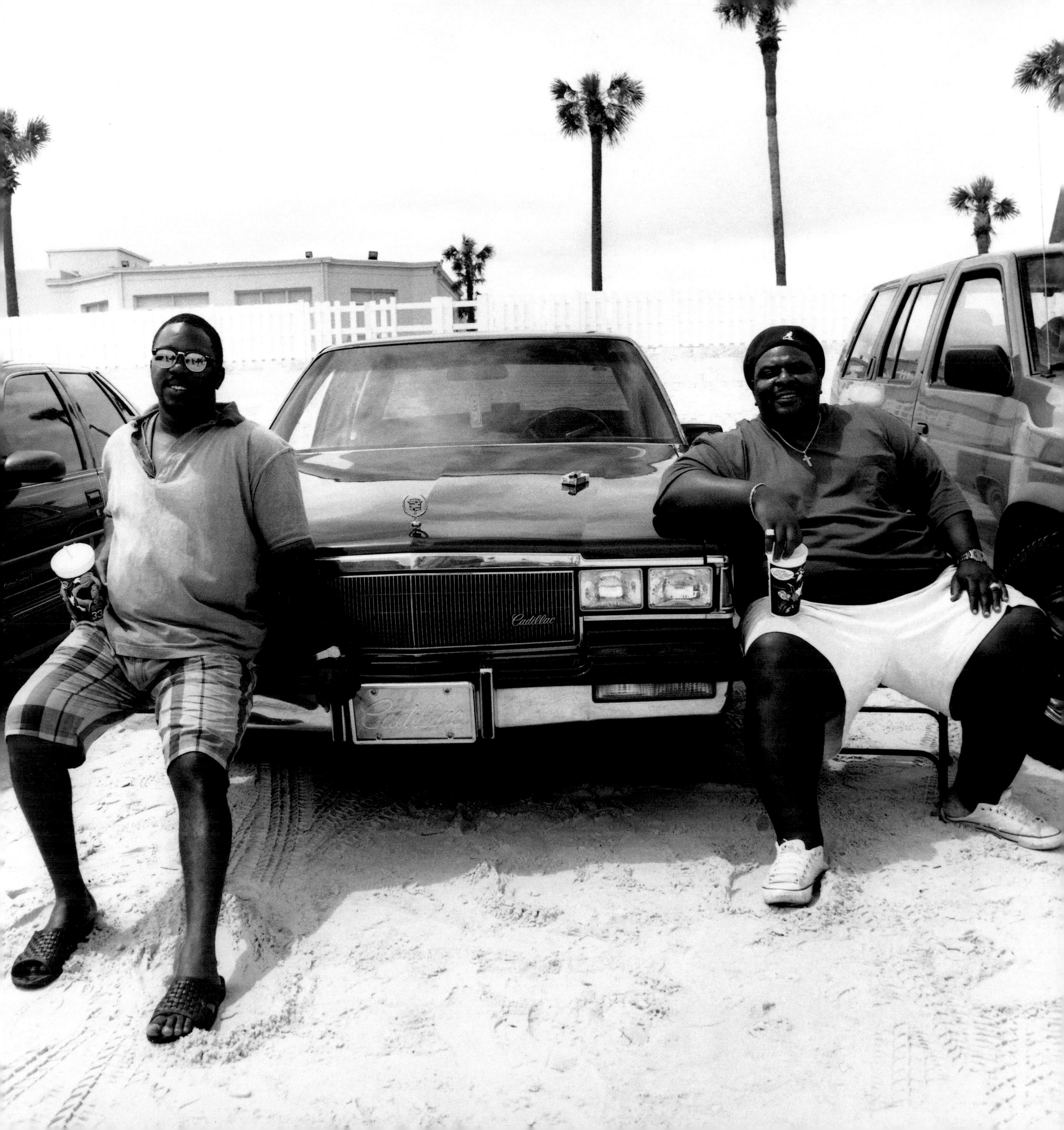
Cadillac
Cadillac

Public school playground,
Washington, D.C., **1995**

The dream of a quick buck.
Mural in East Los Angeles, California, **1993**

Forty-Seventh Street, the diamond-lovers' paradise,
New York City, **1995**

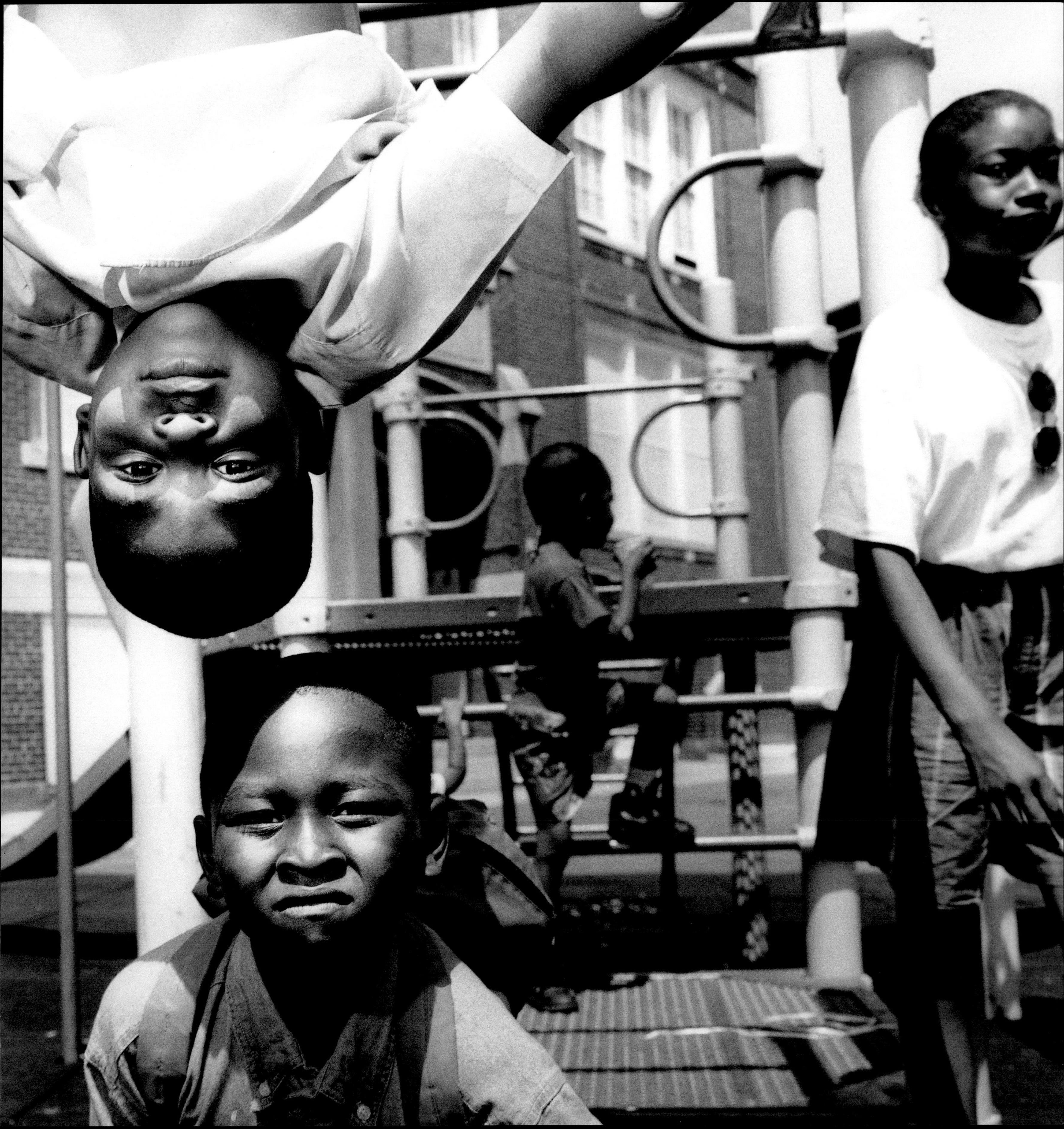

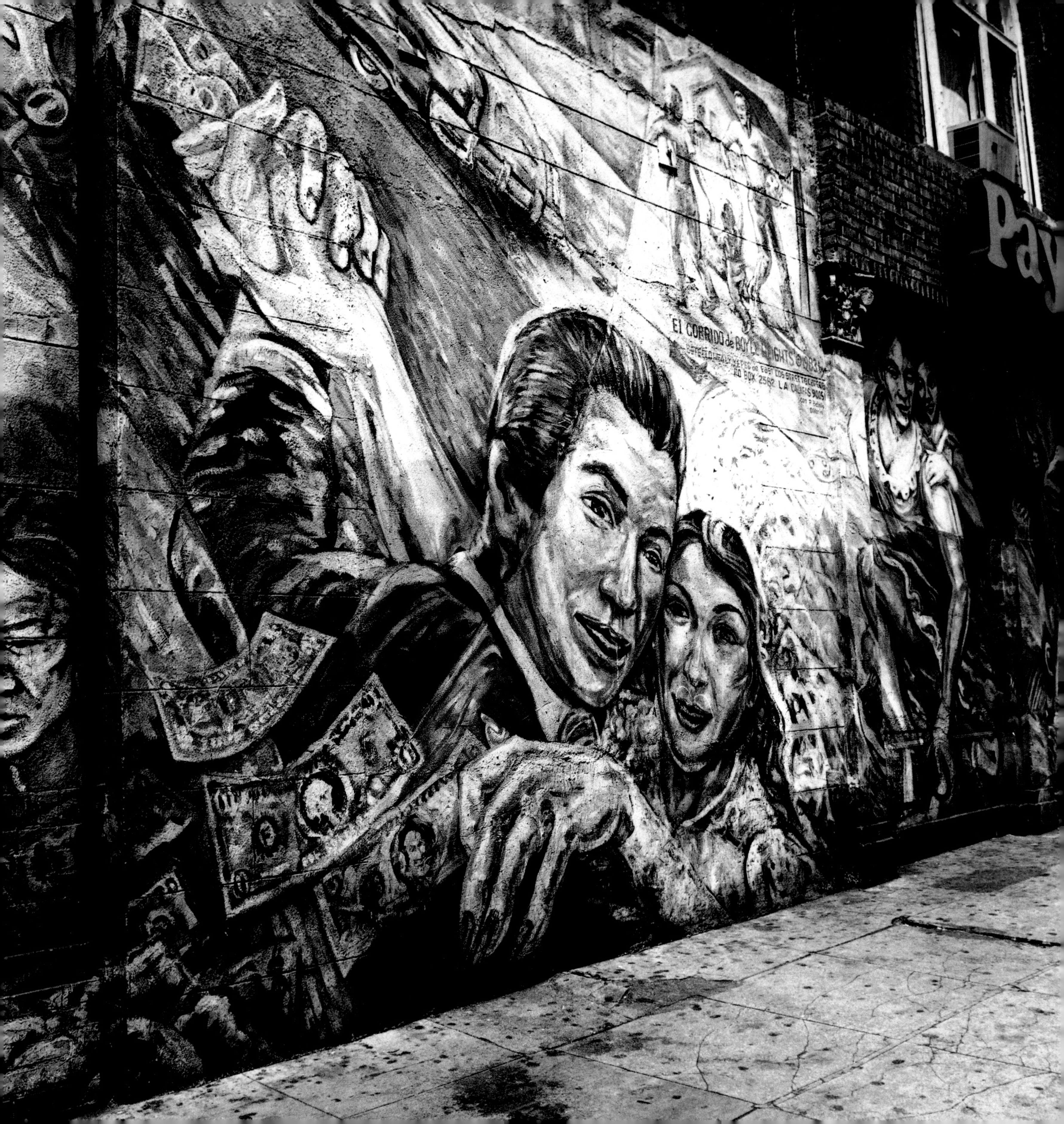
El CORRIDO de
BOX 2582 LA CALIFAS 90051
Pay

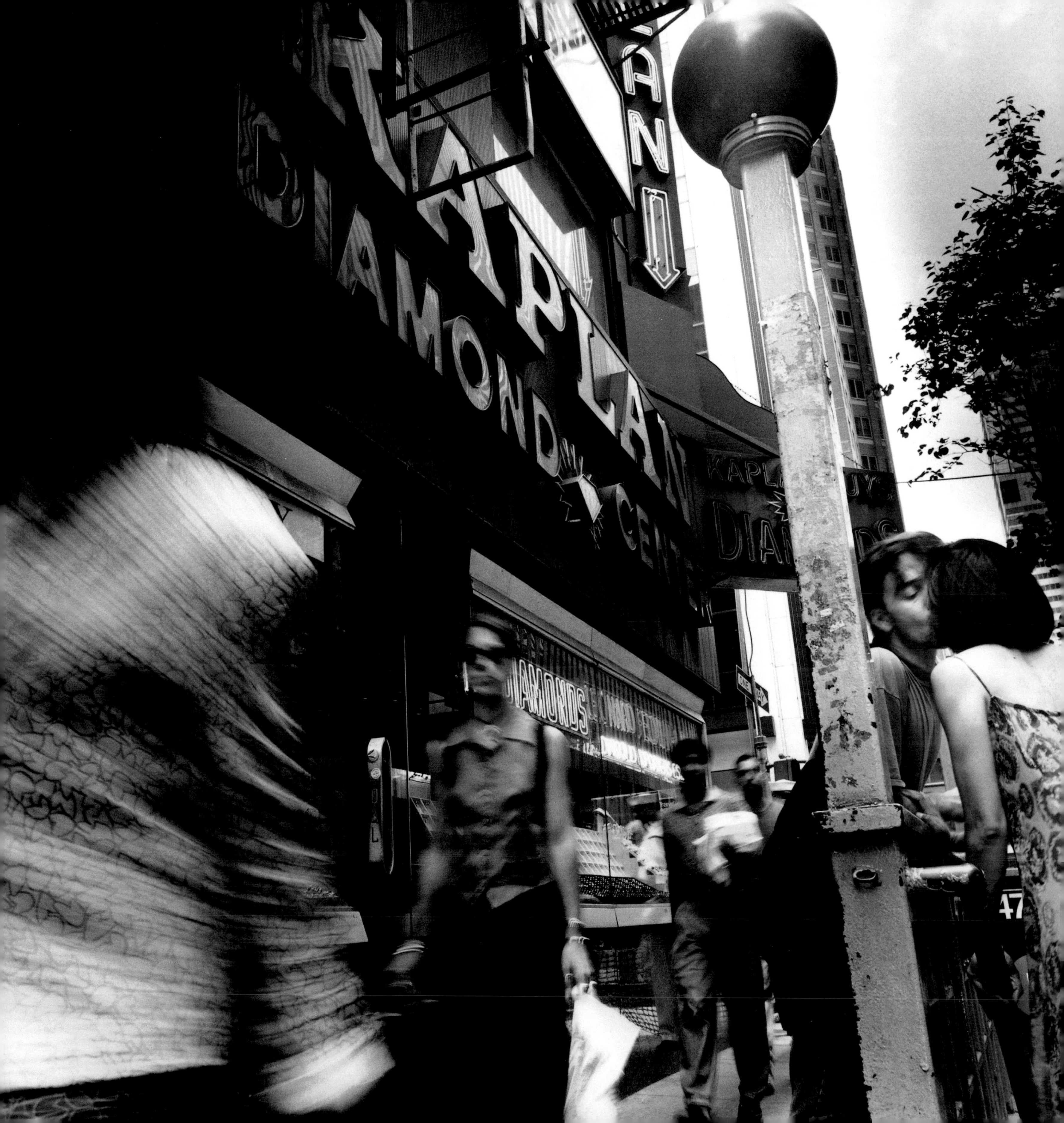
DIAMONDS
47

Trophy shop, Reno, Nevada, **1995**

Cheerleaders practicing for their performance on Independence Day,
Southampton, New York, **1996**

Video games in the Greyhound bus station,
Las Vegas, Nevada, **1995**

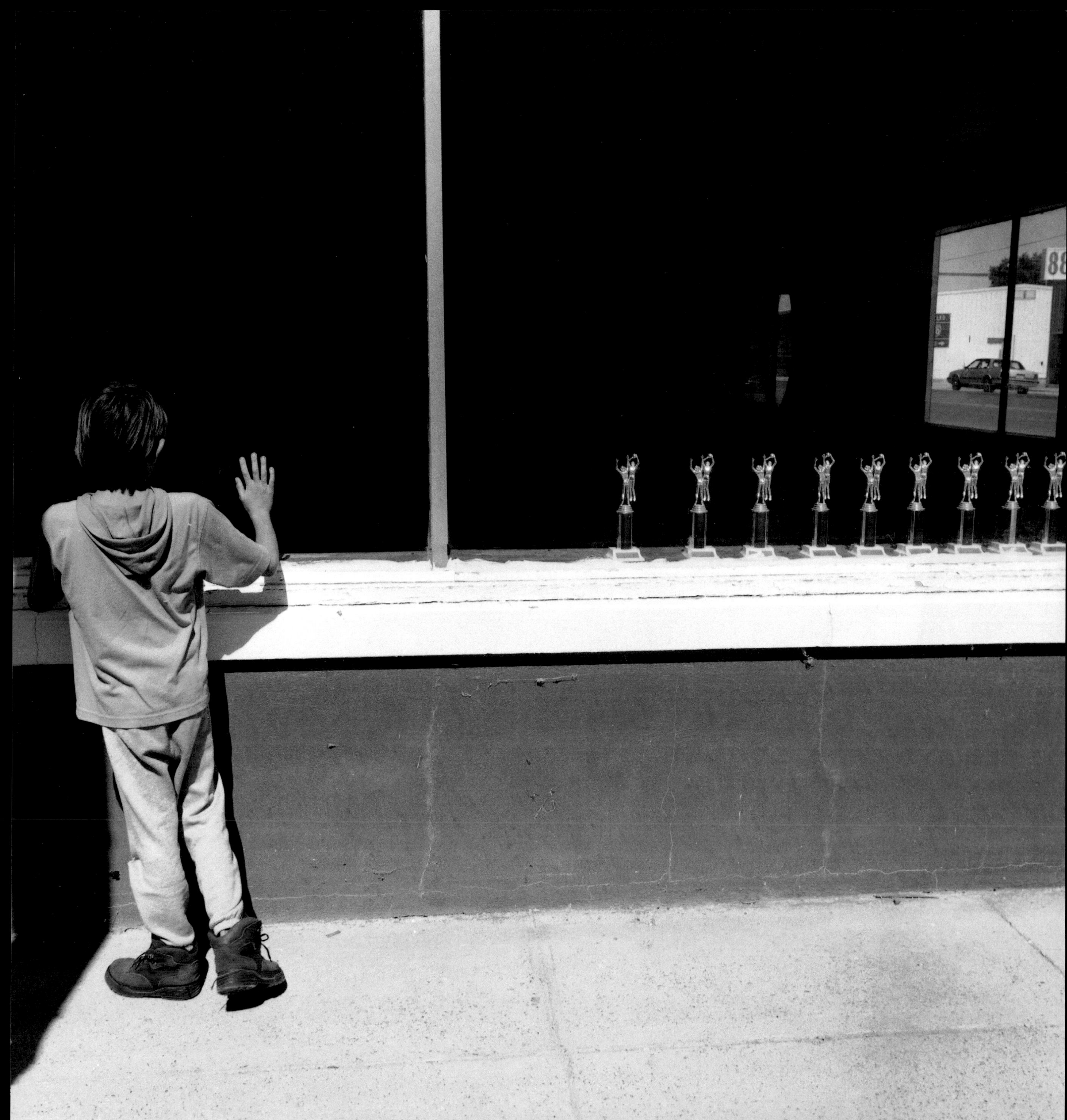

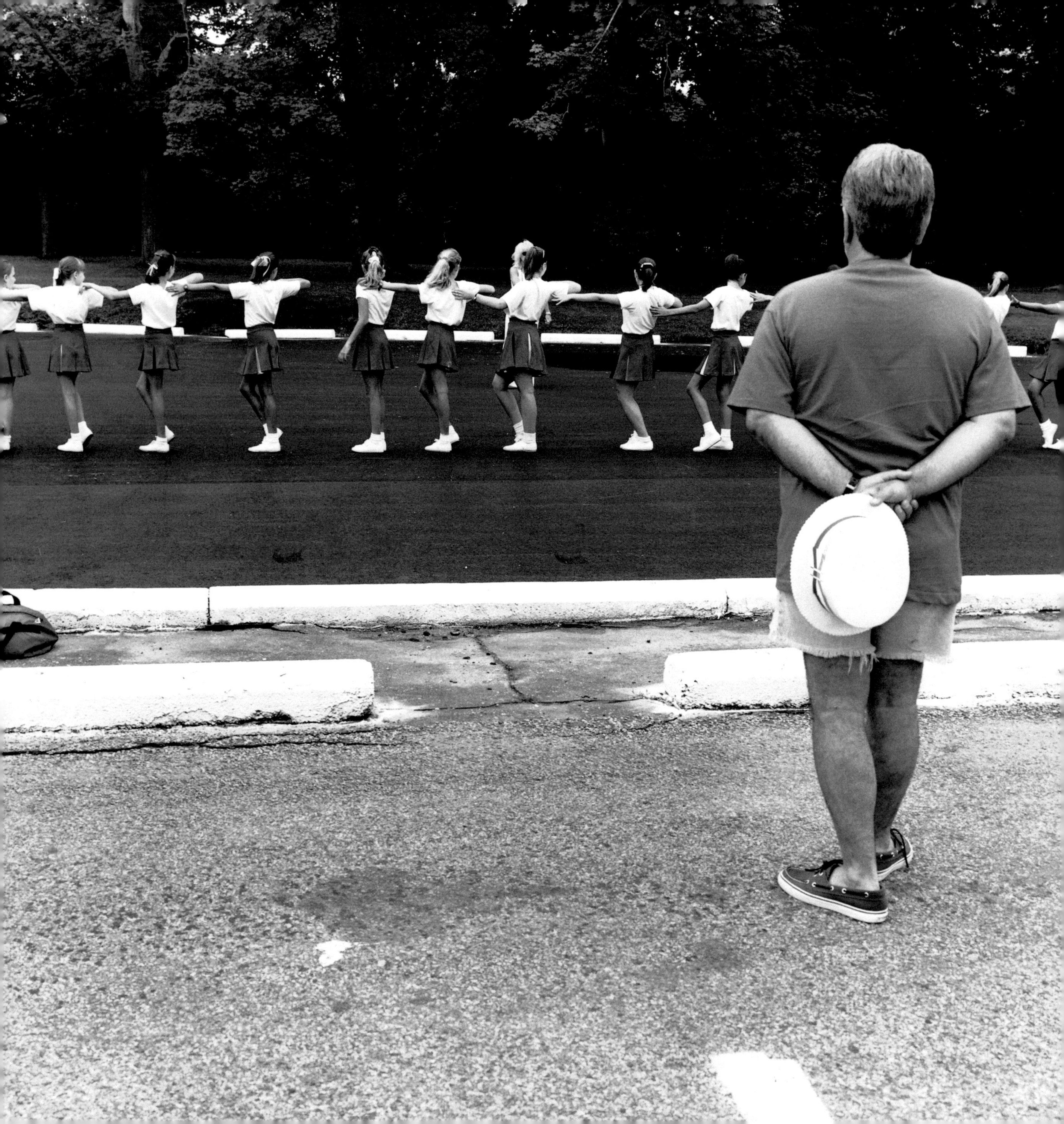

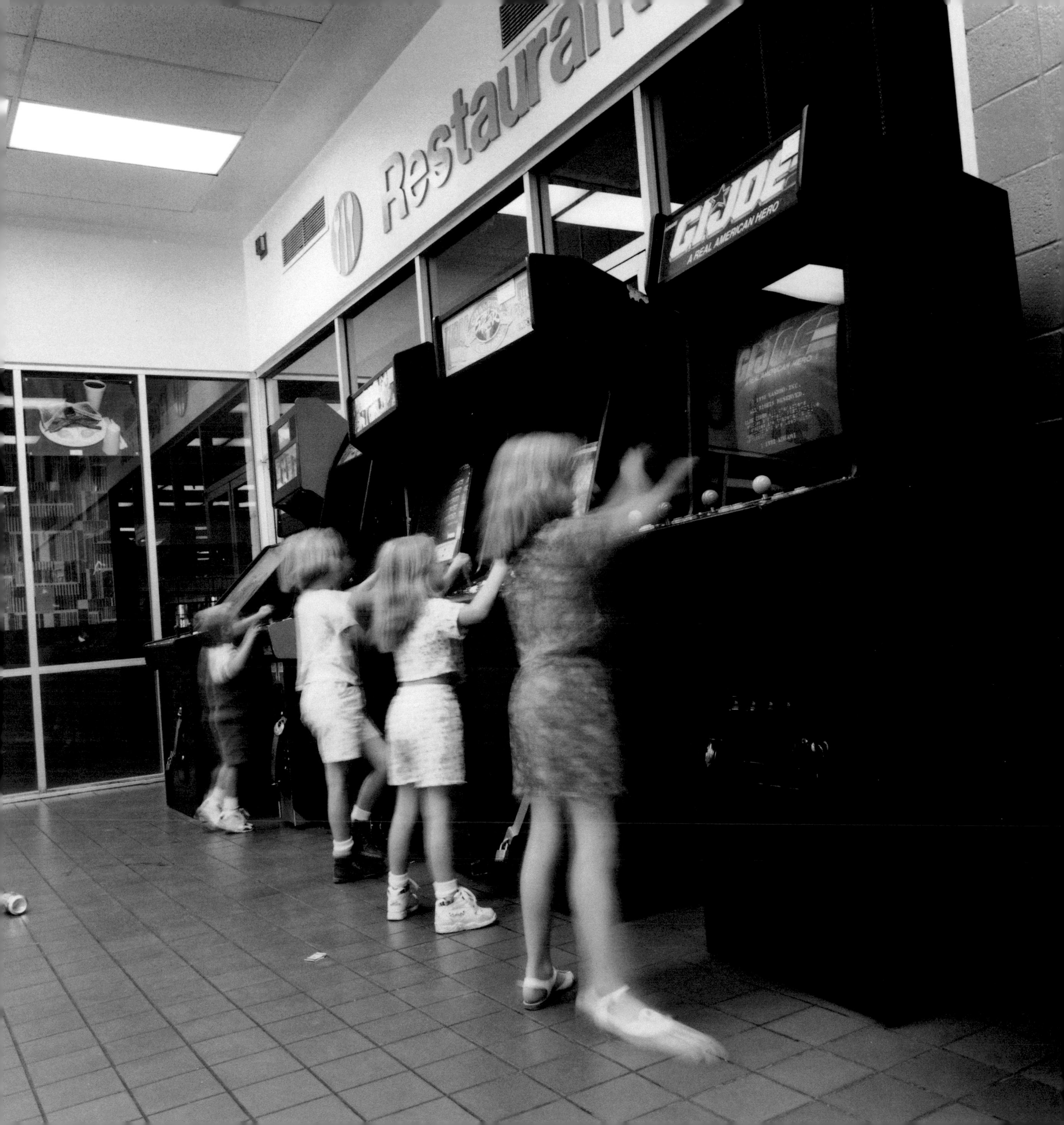
Restauran
GI JOE
A REAL AMERICAN HERO

Thanksgiving Day Parade,
New York City, **1995**

Welfare ball. Celine with her adopted
daughters in the Beverly Wiltshire Hotel, Beverly Hills,
California, **1993**

Washington Square Park,
New York City, **1990**

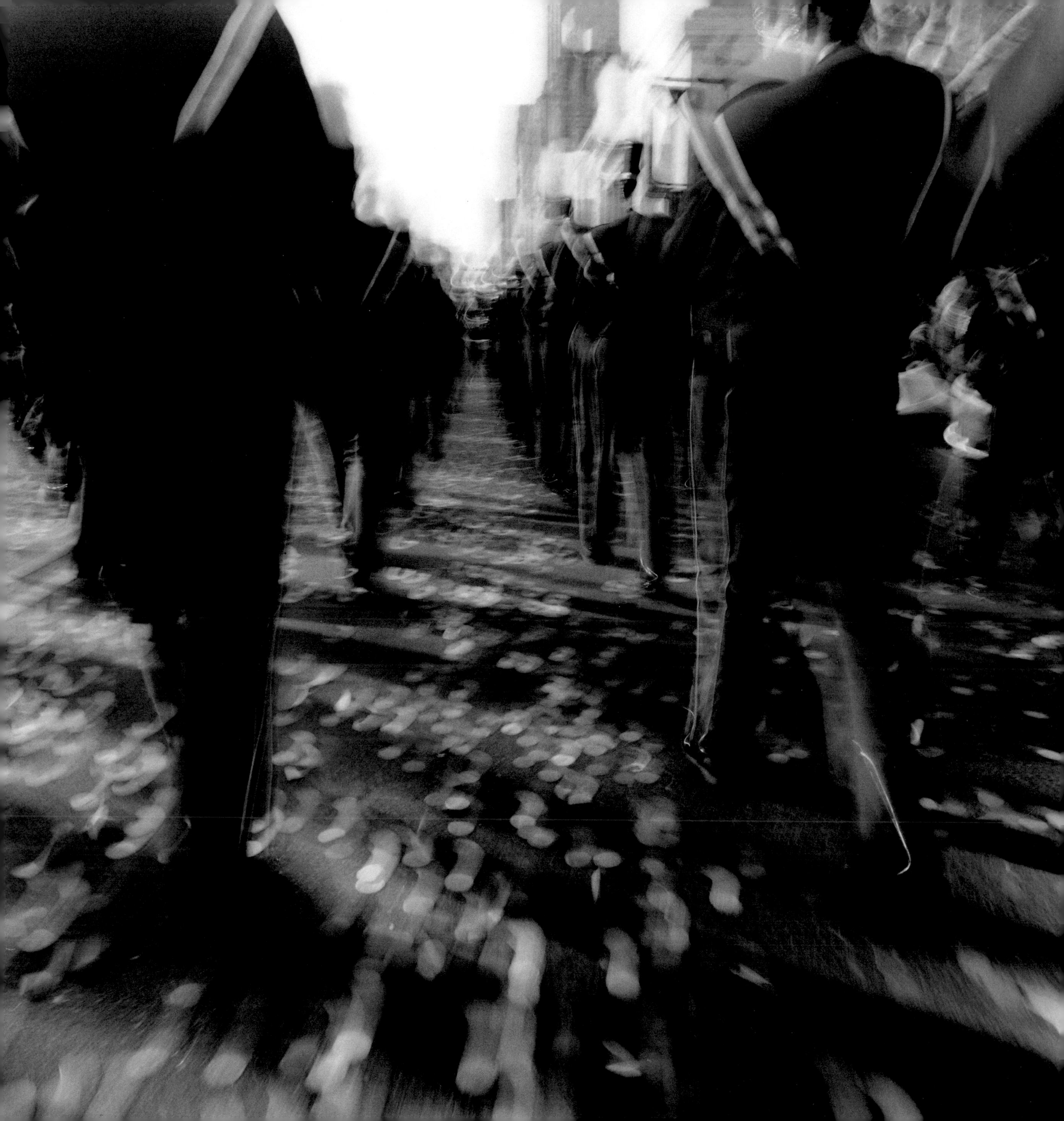

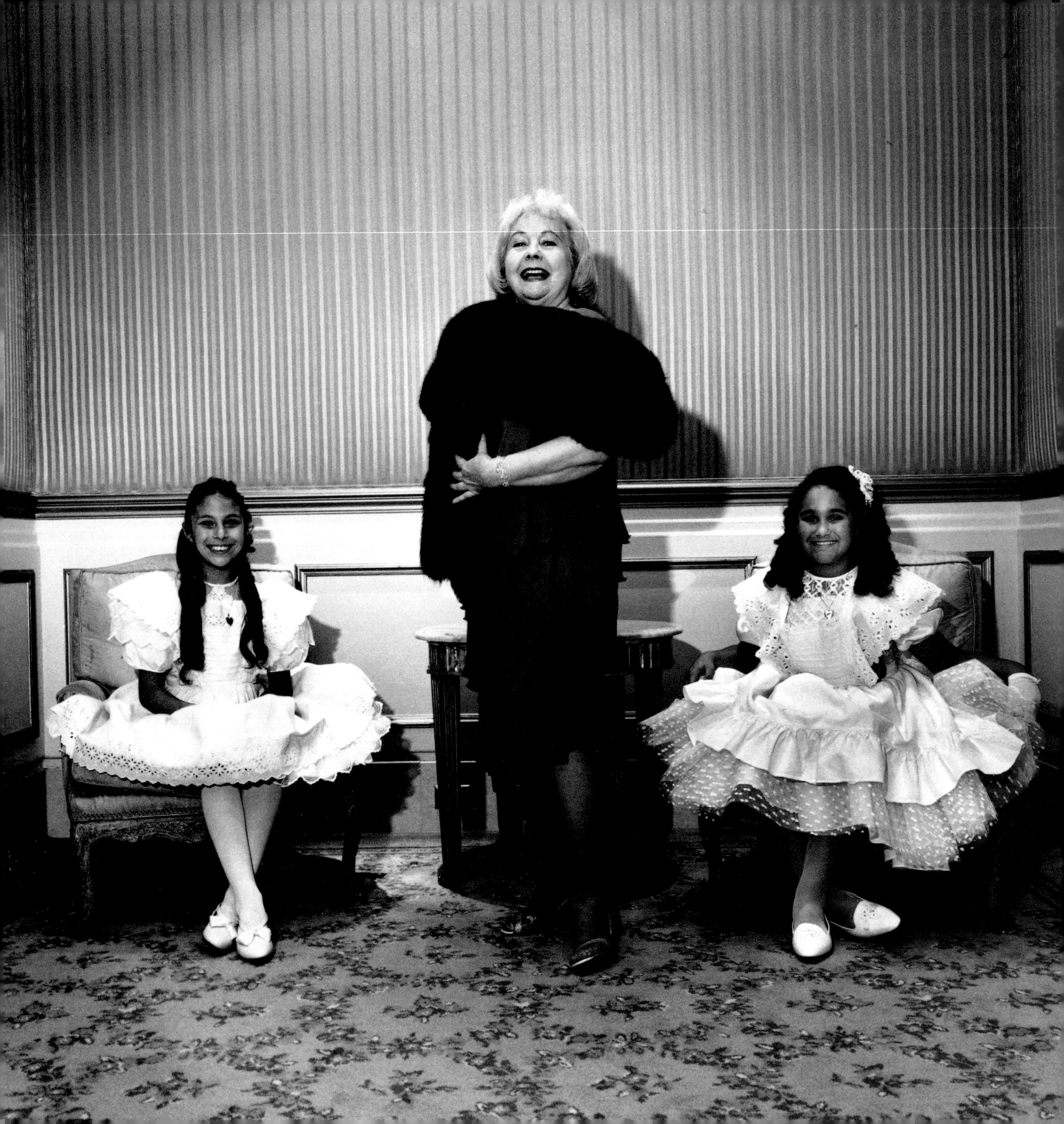

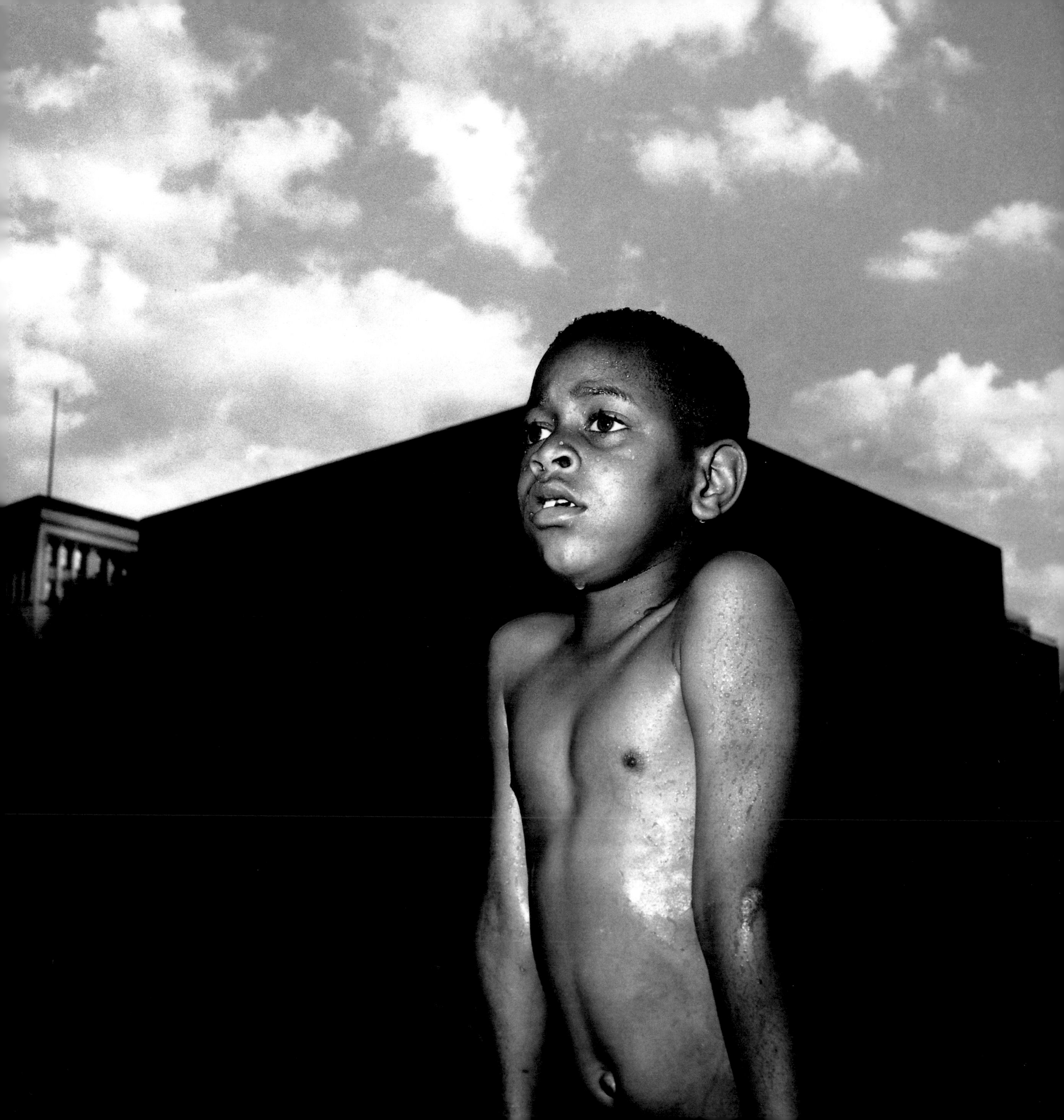

Commuters on the Staten Island Ferry,
New York, **1995**

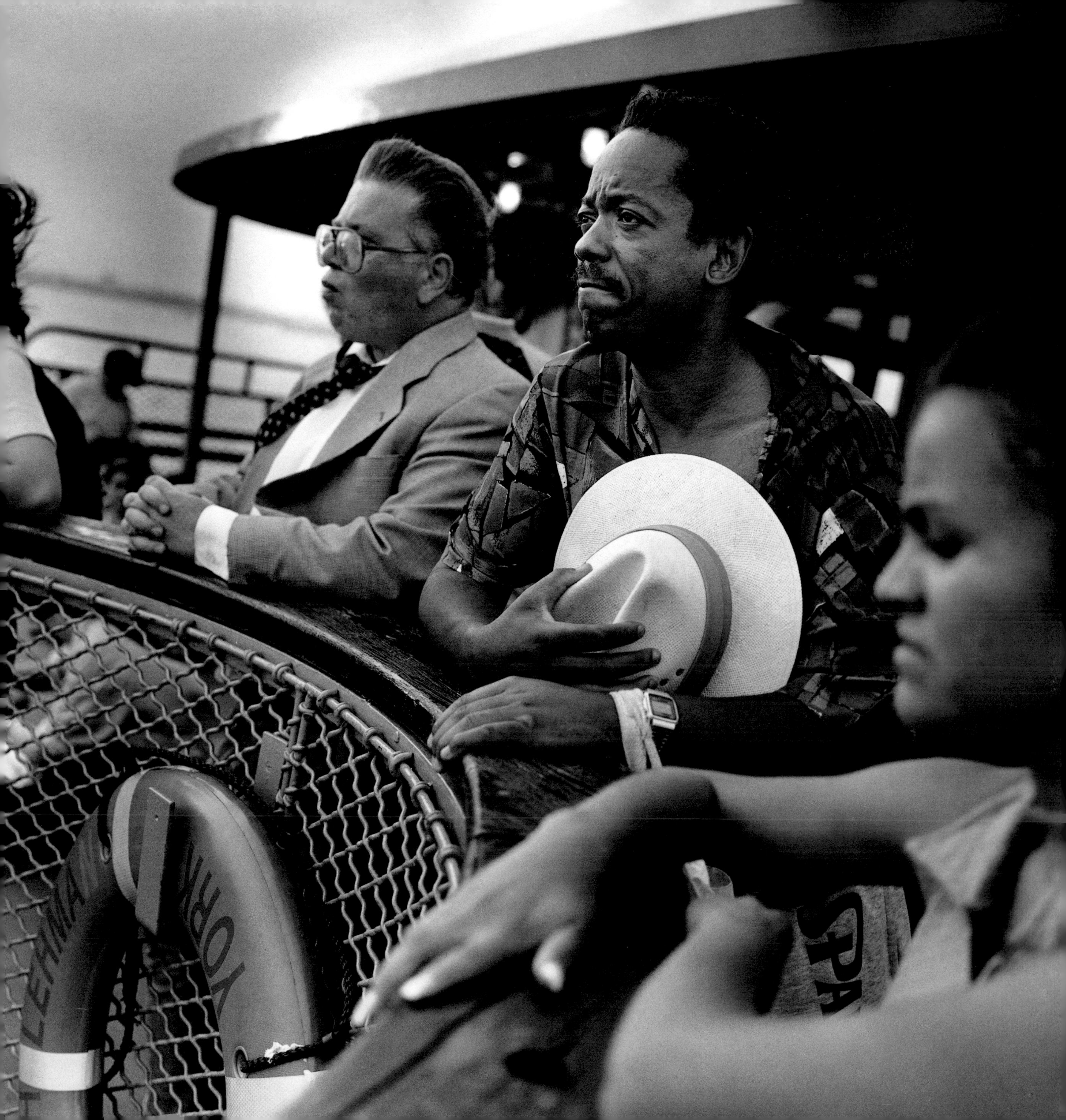
YORK

II.

The Prom, a big night for high-school graduates,
Montauk, New York, **1996**

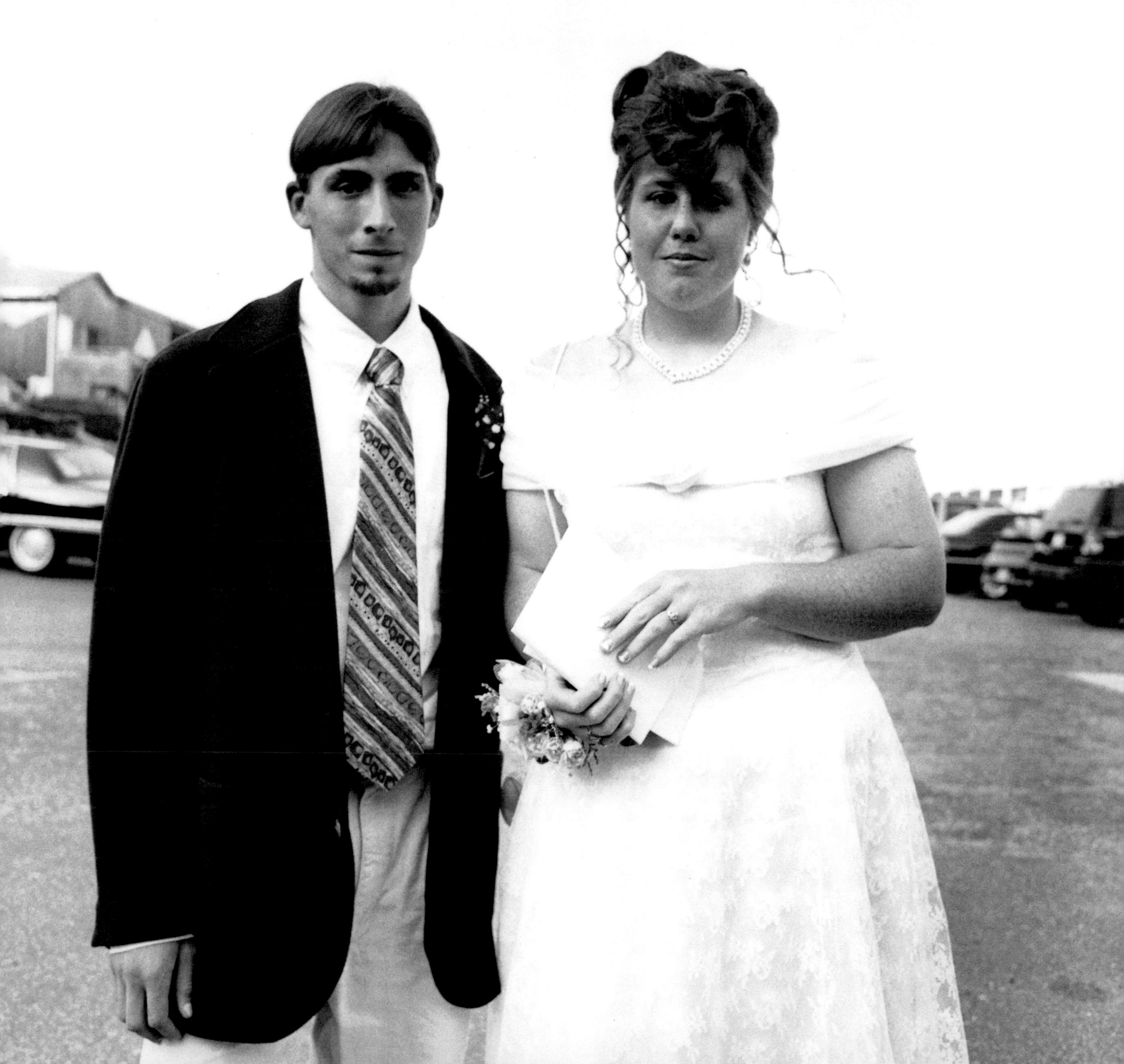

The Prom, a big night for high-school graduates,
Southampton, New York, **1996**

Showcase window of an empty beauty salon,
Washington, D.C., **1995**

Hairstylist's shop specializing in artificial hair braiding,
Washington, D.C., **1995**

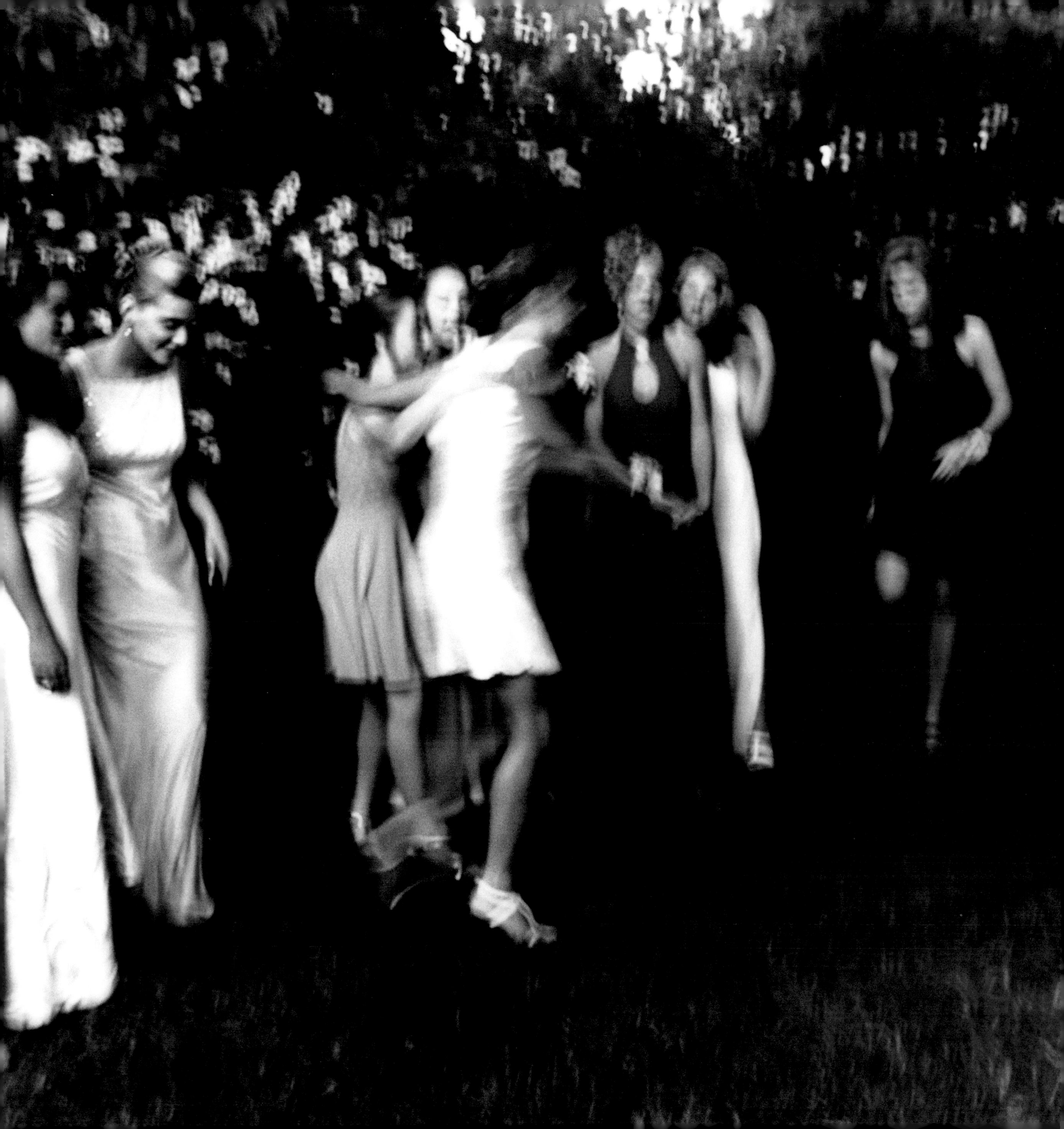

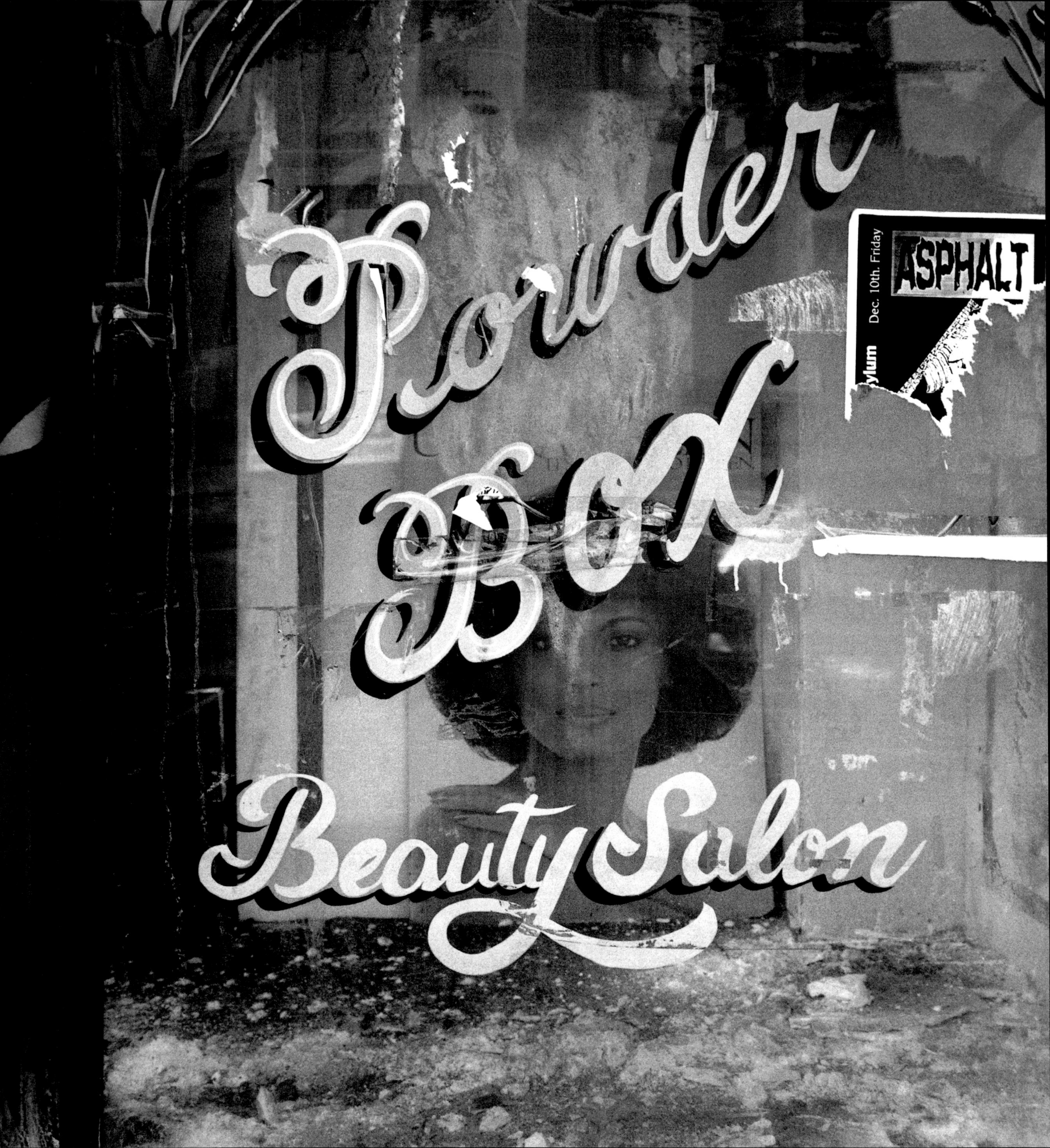

Powder
Box
Beauty Salon

ASPHALT
Dec. 10th. Friday
ylum

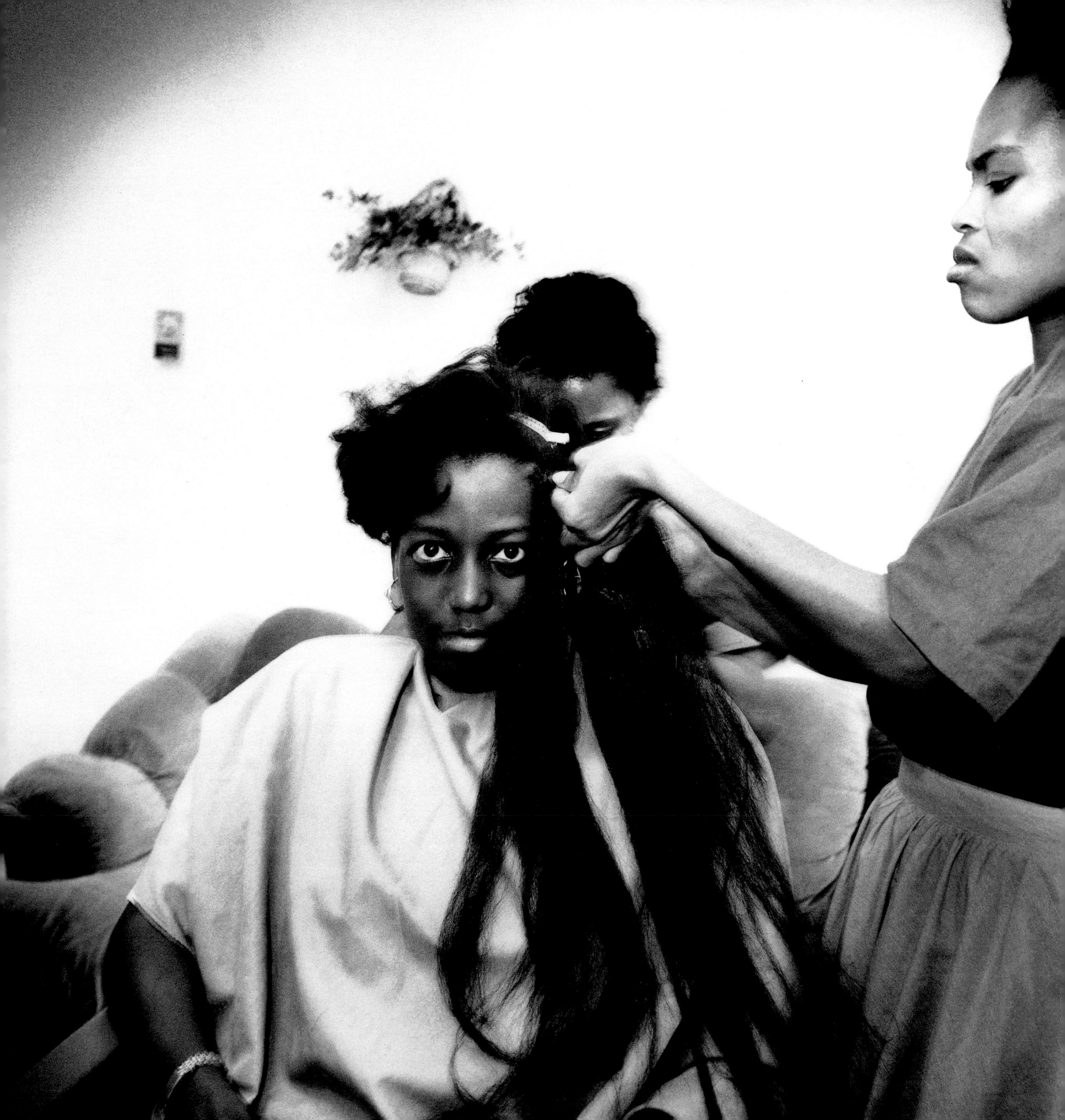

Polish barber shop, Greenpoint,
New York, **1990**

Portrait of a candy shop owner and his family,
Hollywood, California, **1994**

Wax figure cabinet, Branson,
Missouri, **1993**

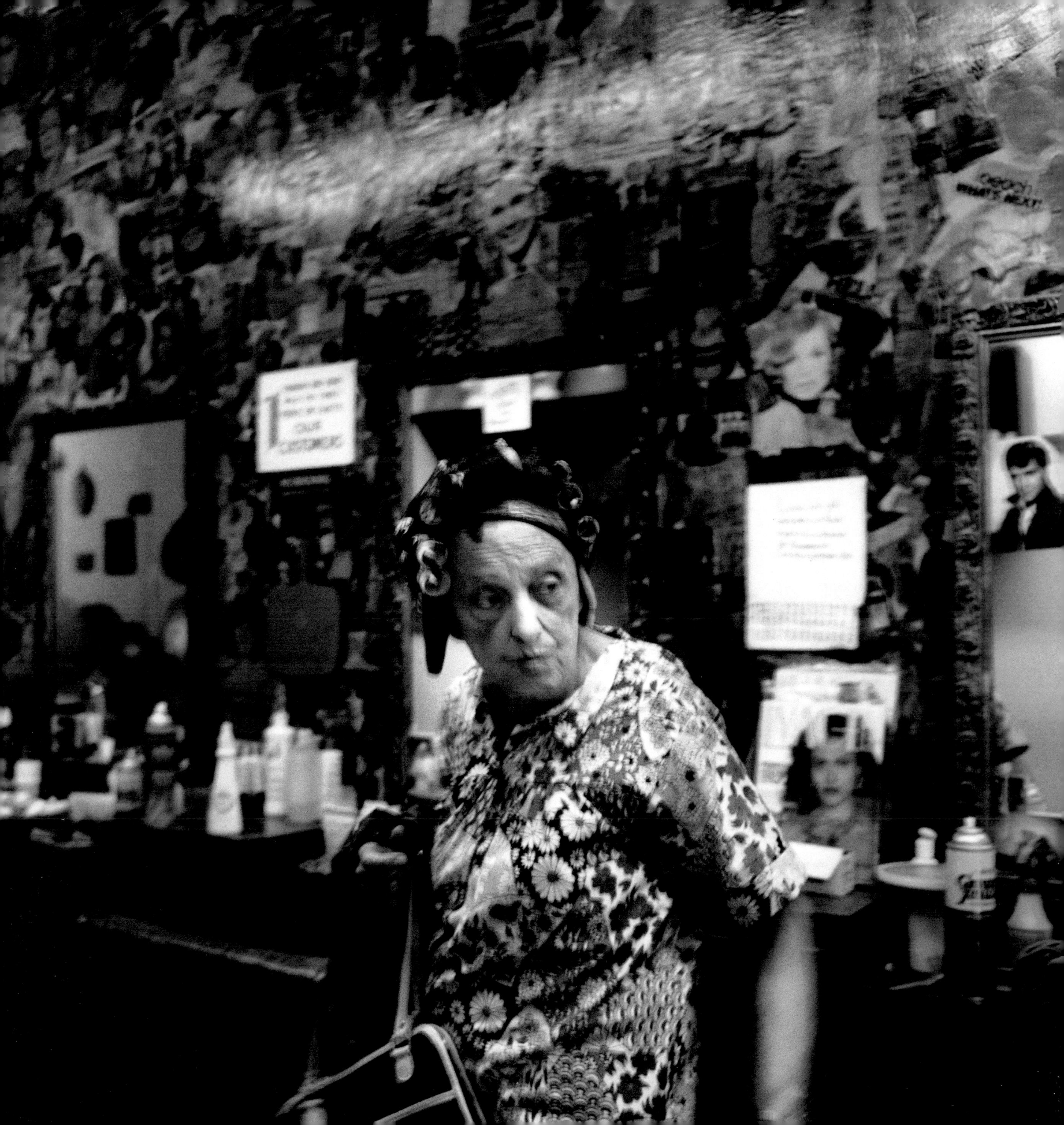

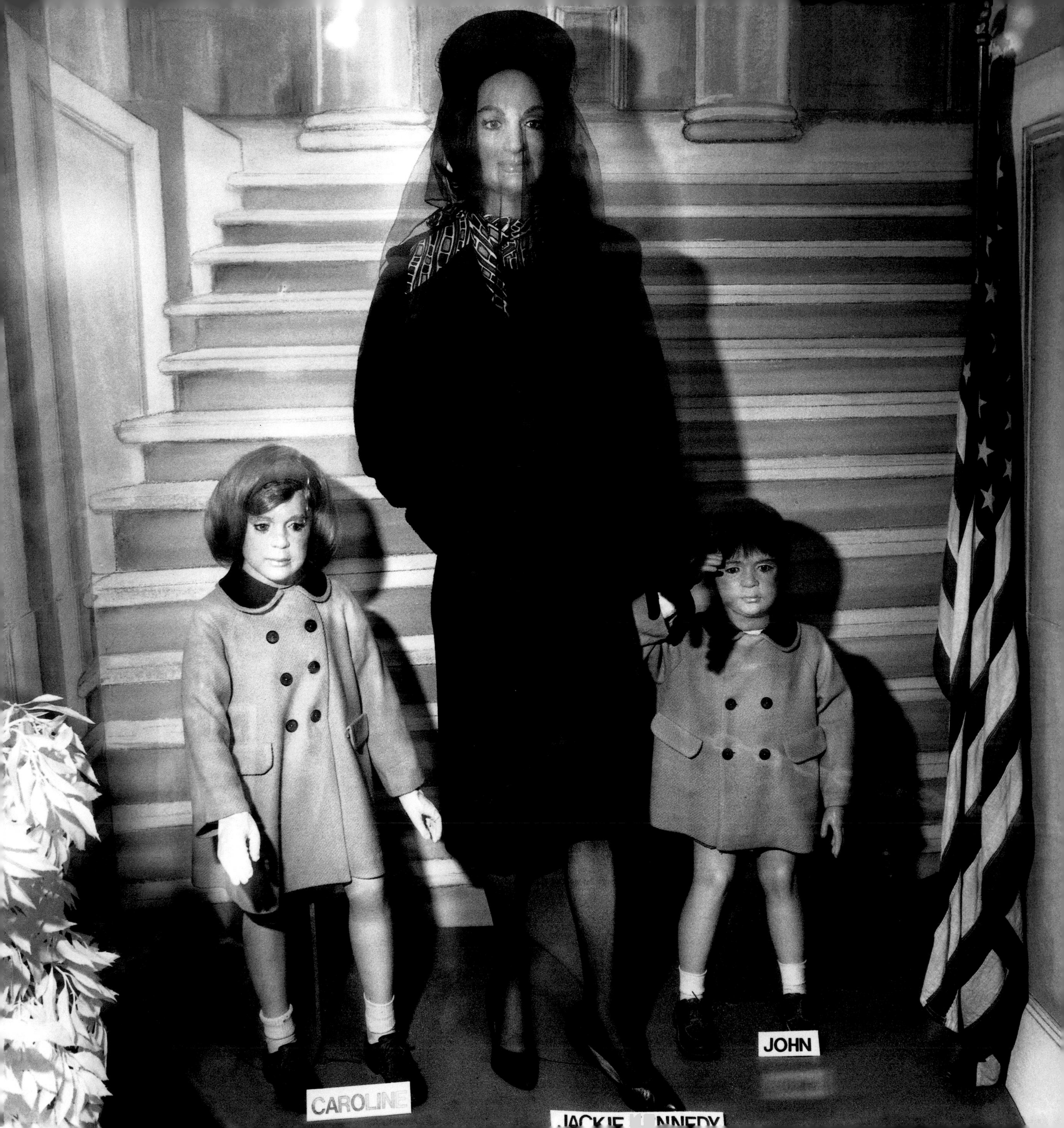
JOHN
CAROLINE

John F. Kennedy's grave, Arlington, Virginia, **1995**

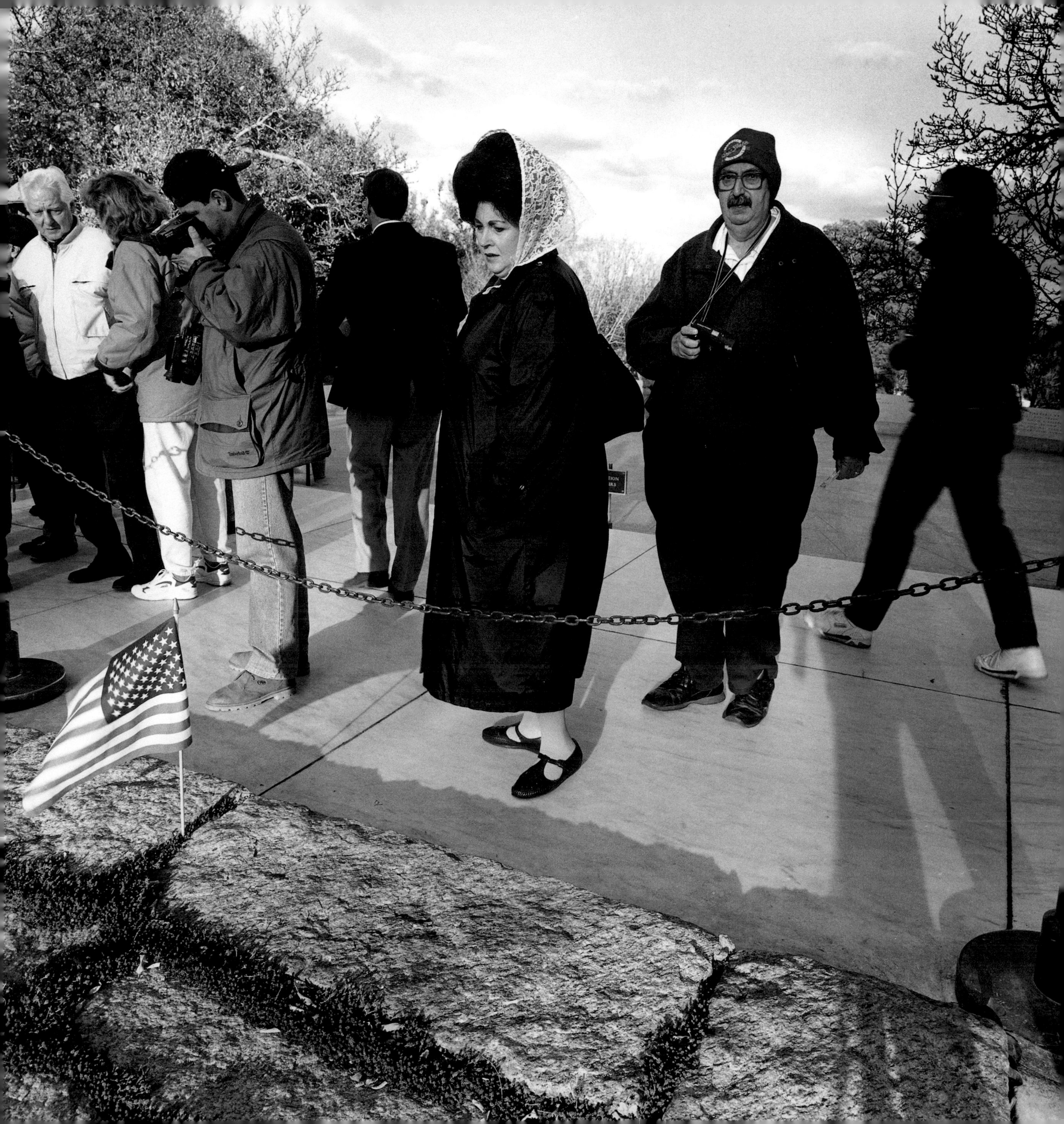

Maids in the Beverly Wiltshire Hotel,
Beverly Hills, California, **1994**

"Miss Olympia," a body-building competition for women,
Chicago, Illinois, **1996**

Woman at a country-and-western concert,
Branson, Missouri, **1993**

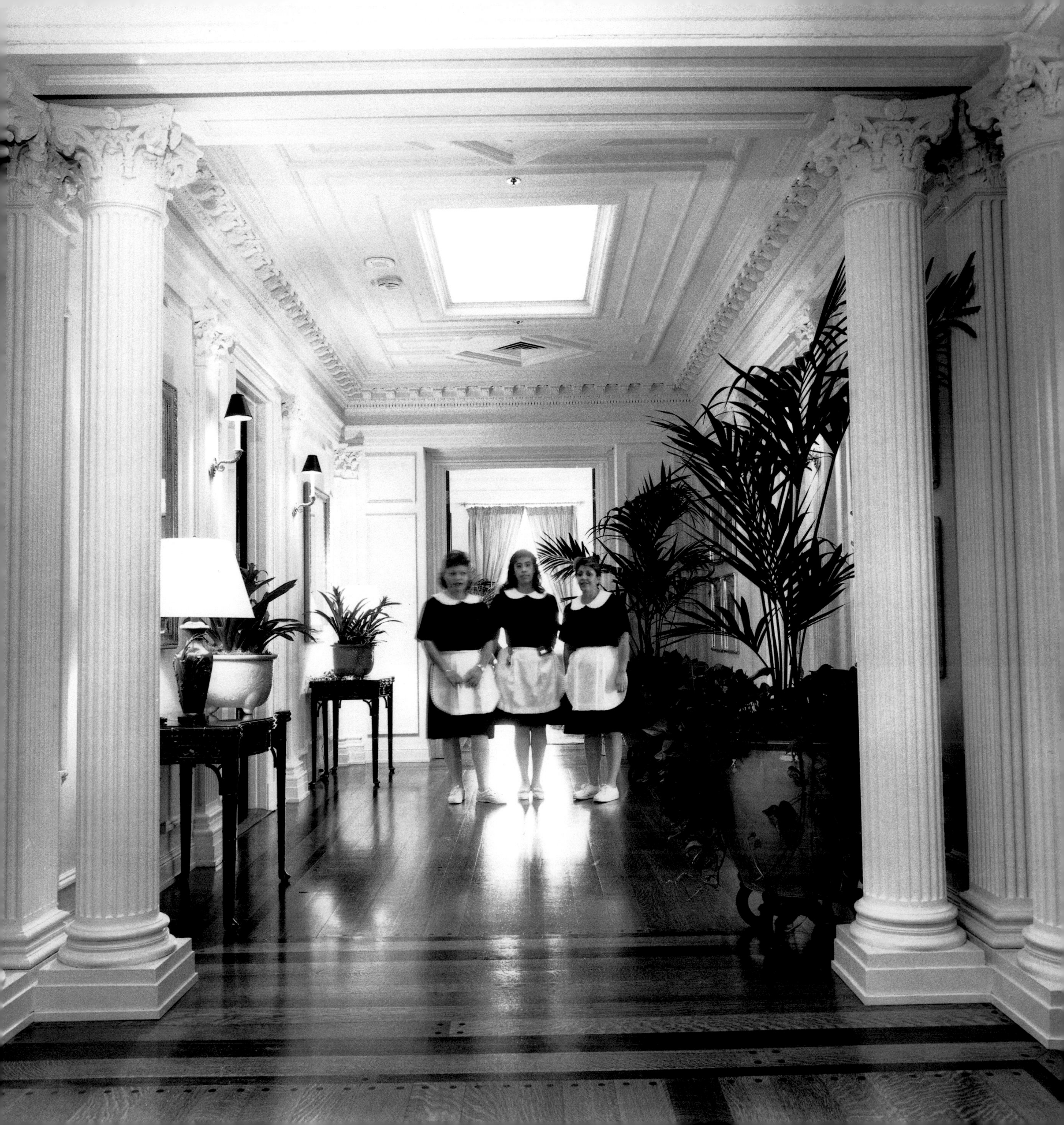

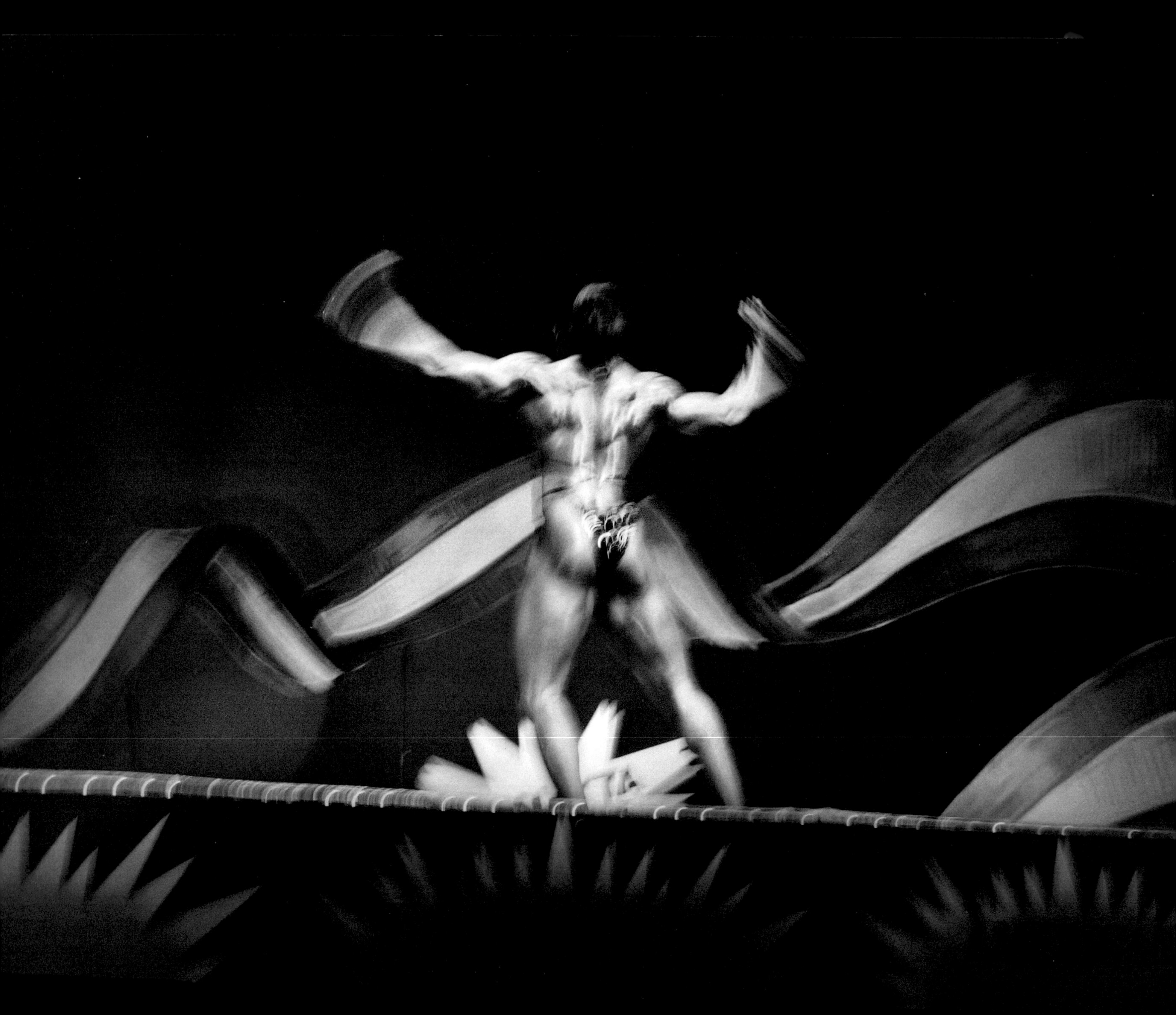

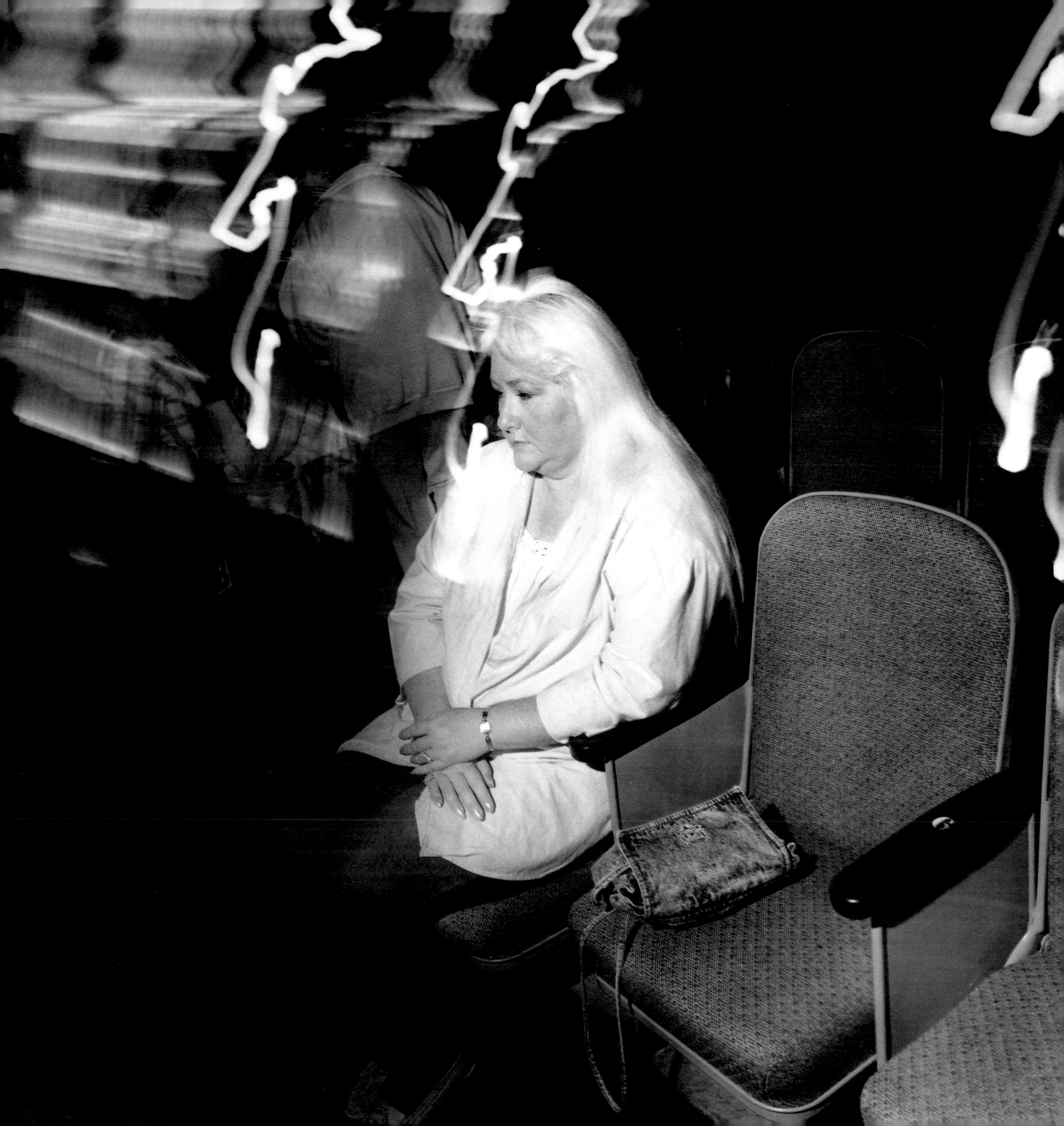

Elvis fan, Greenpoint, New York, **1987**

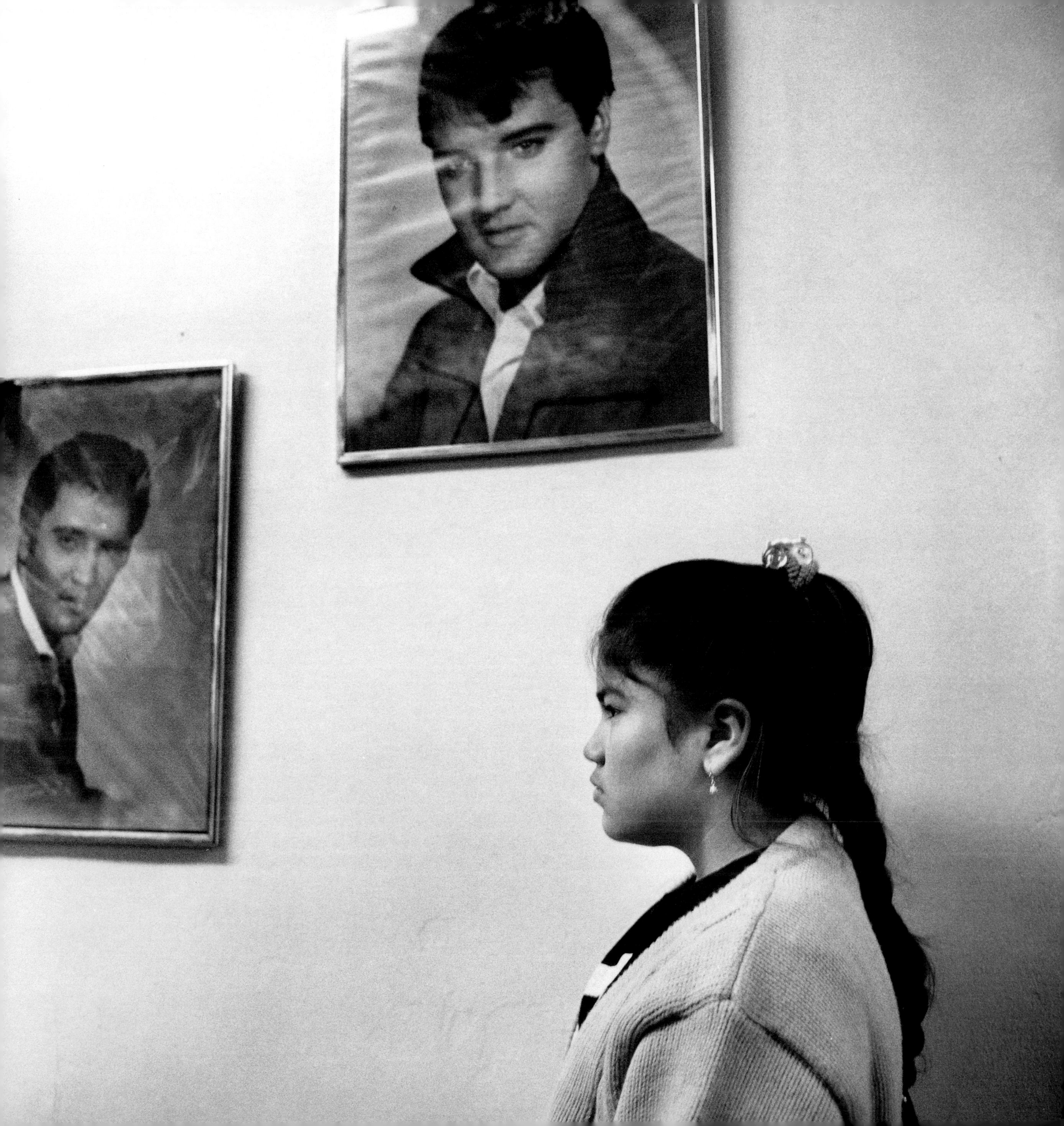

Hollywood real estate agent,
Beverly Hills, California, **1994**

Last-minute preparations for a marriage
ceremony in the sacristy of the Church of St. John the Divine,
New York City, **1996**

The wedding of Jenny and Holger, Berkshire,
Massachusetts, **1996**

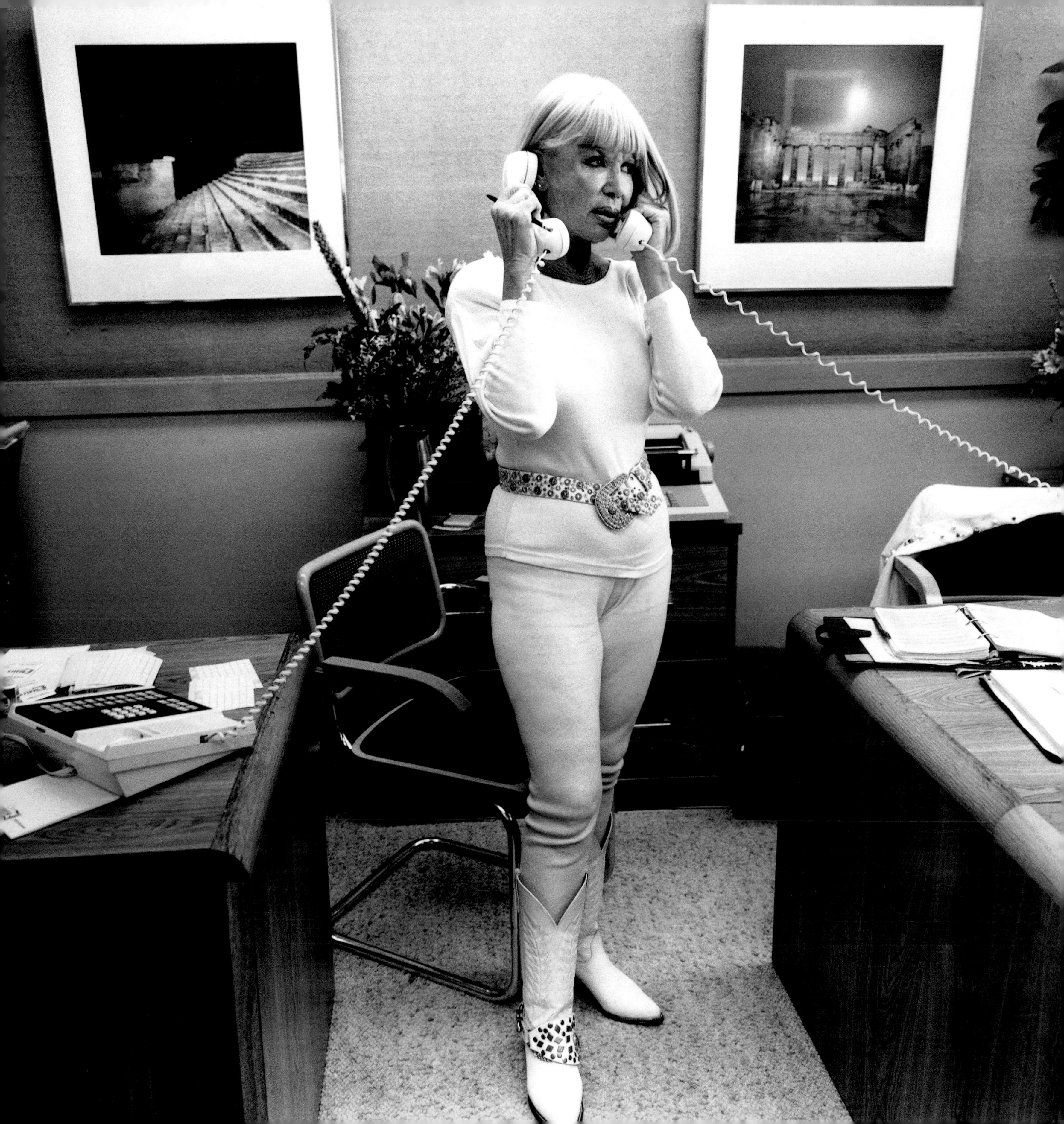

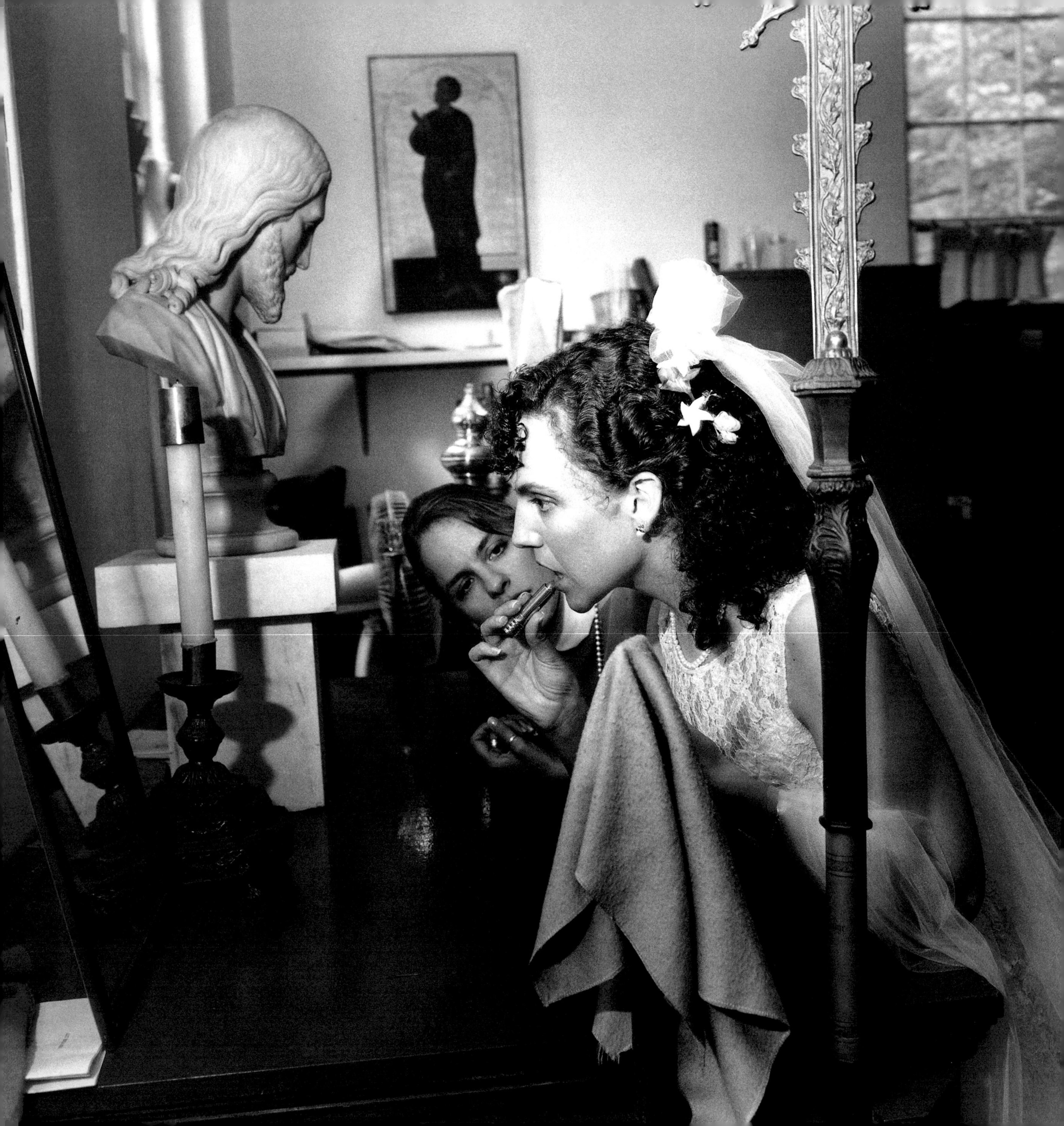

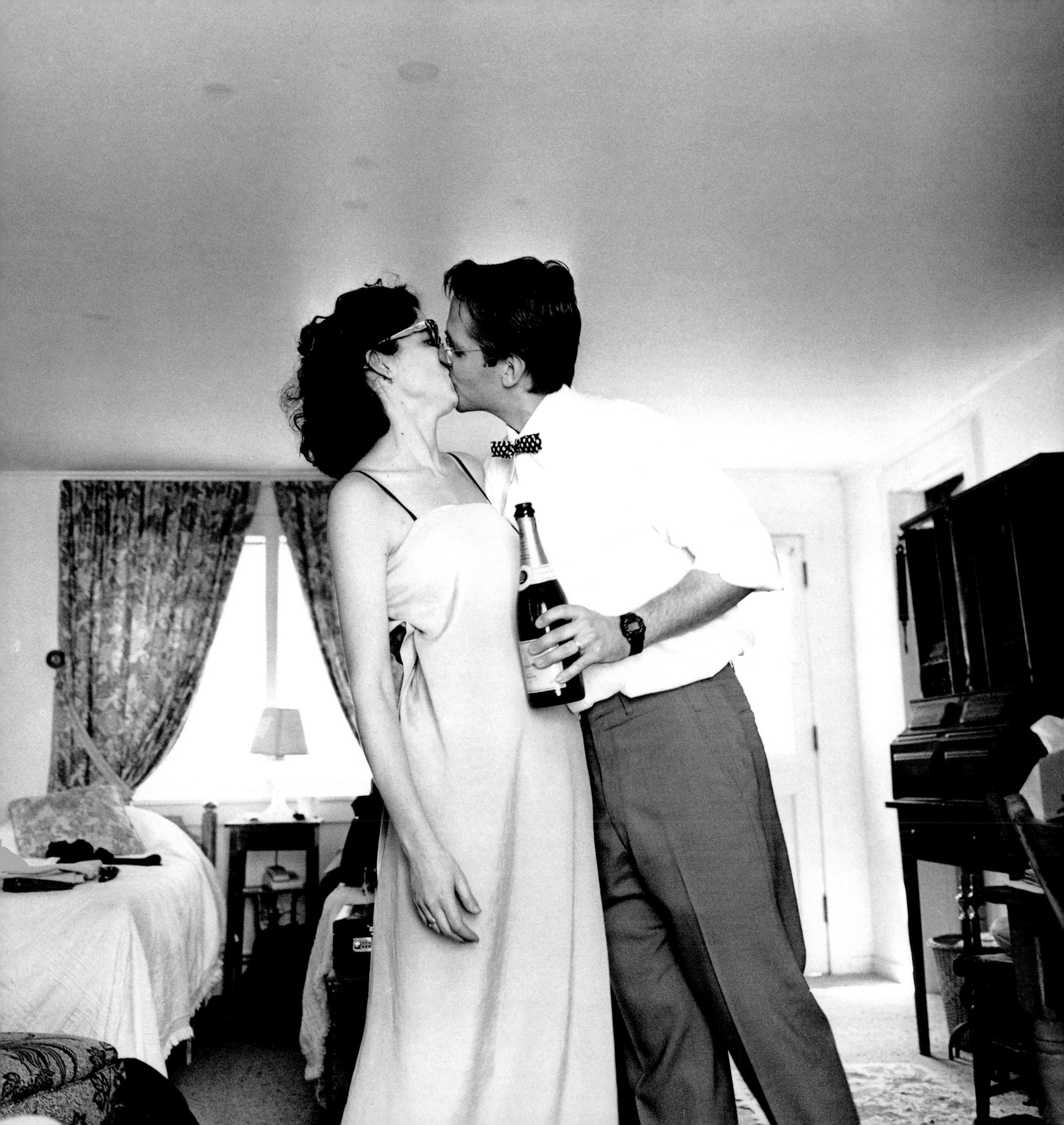

III.

Memorial Day, Arlington, Virginia, **1996**

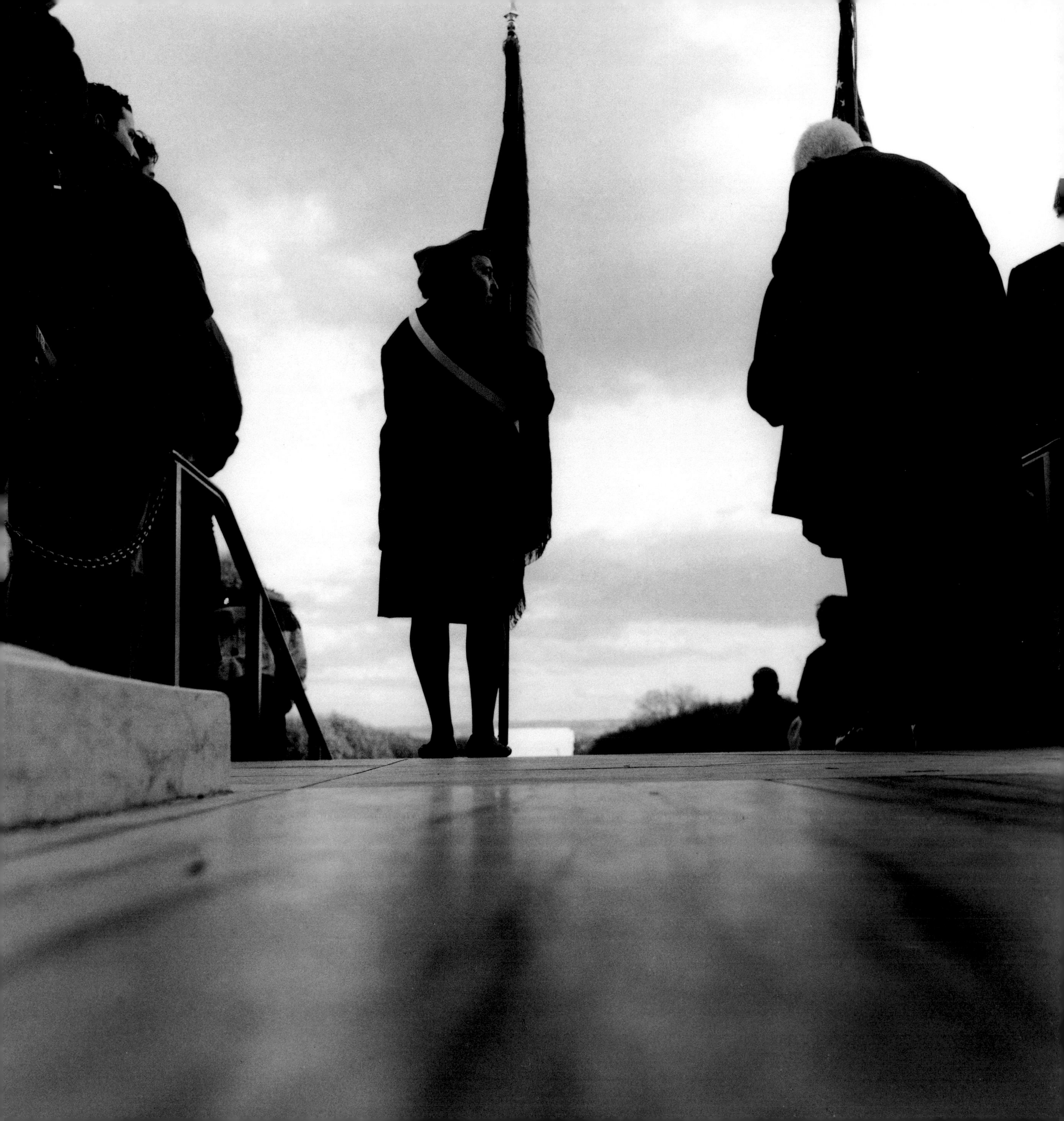

A veteran of three wars at the Vietnam Memorial,
Memorial Day, Washington, D.C.,
1996

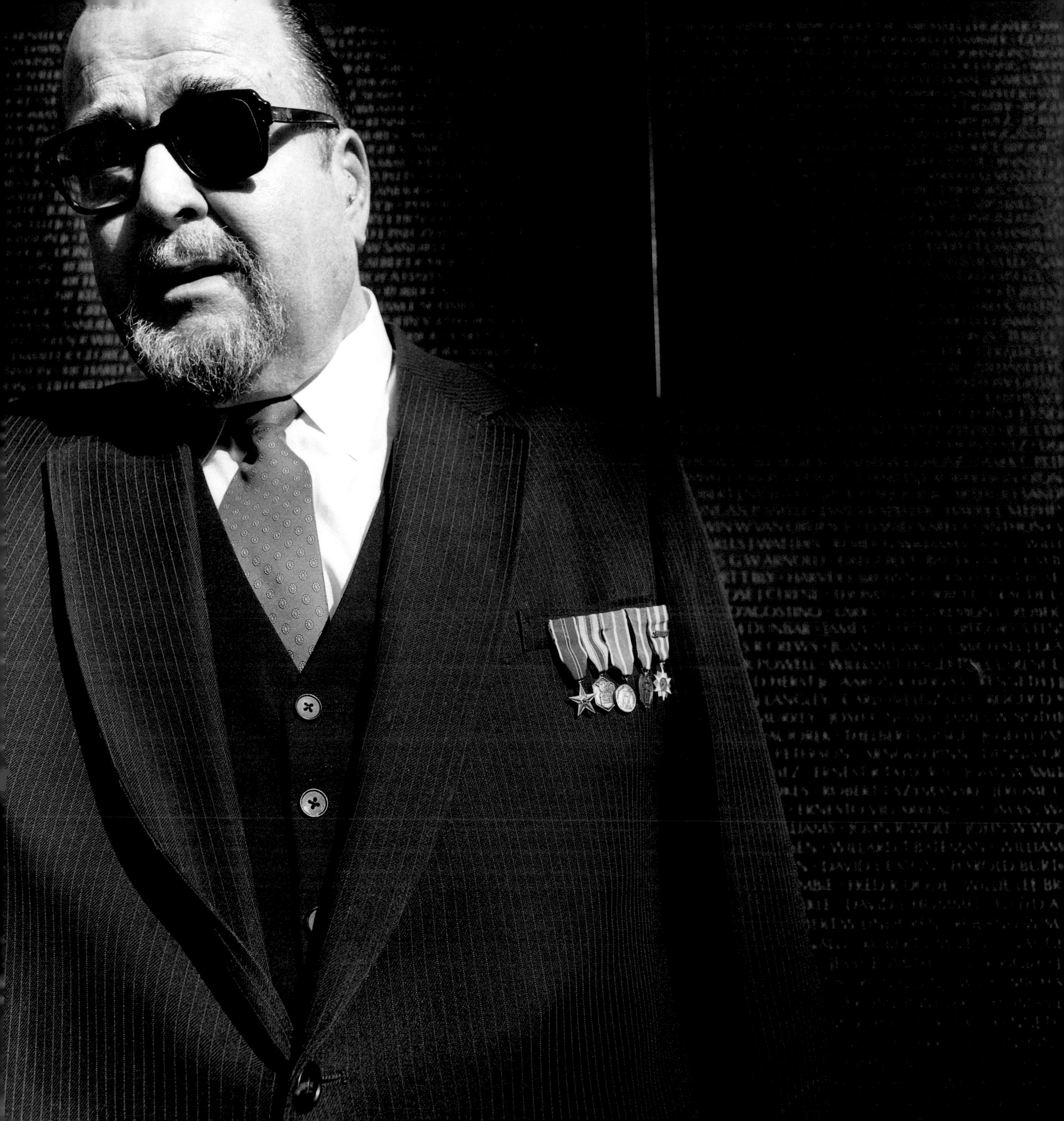

Robert Kennedy's grave, Arlington, Virginia, **1996**

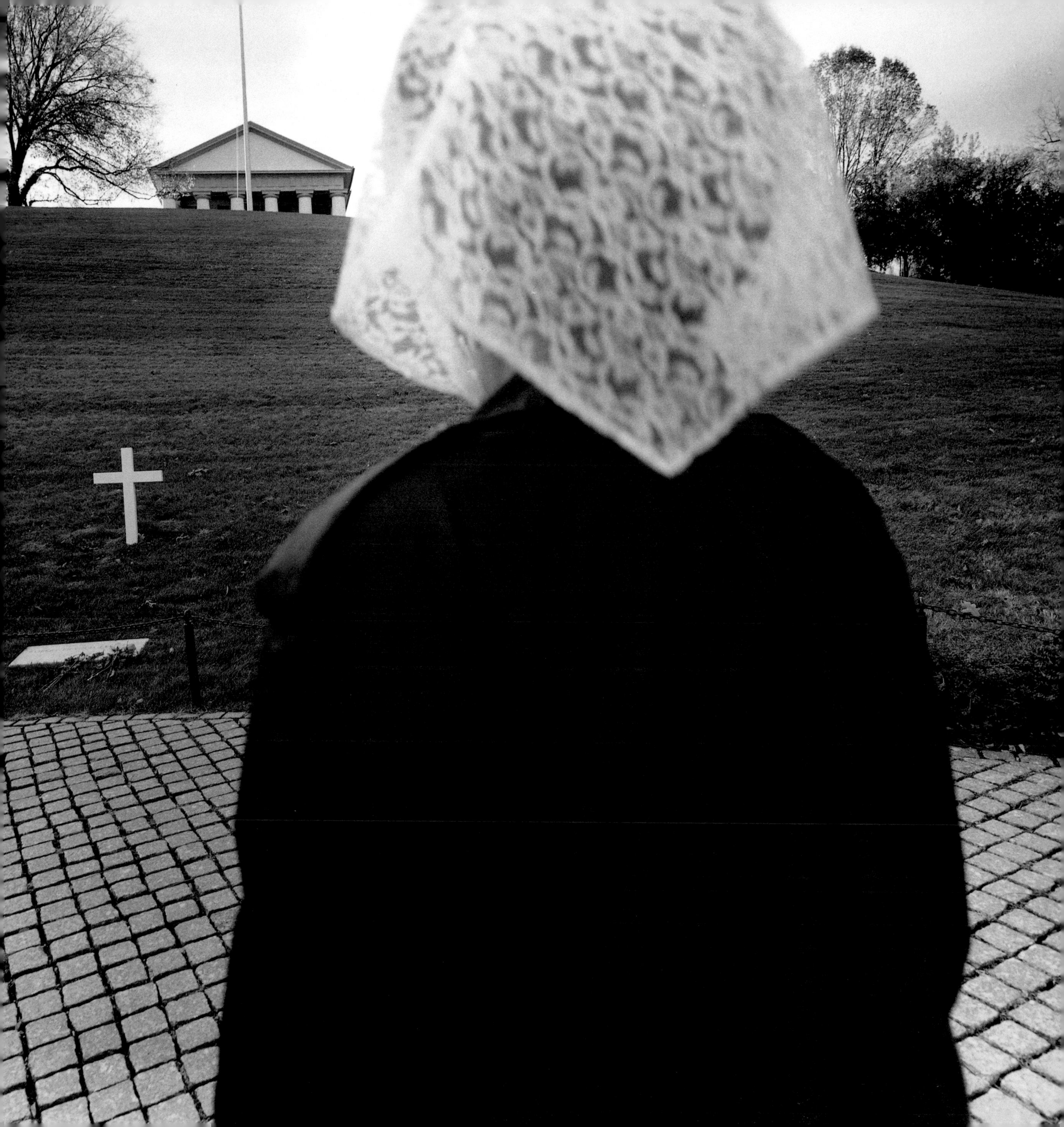

Flags flying in front of homes on Independence Day,
Southampton, New York, **1996**

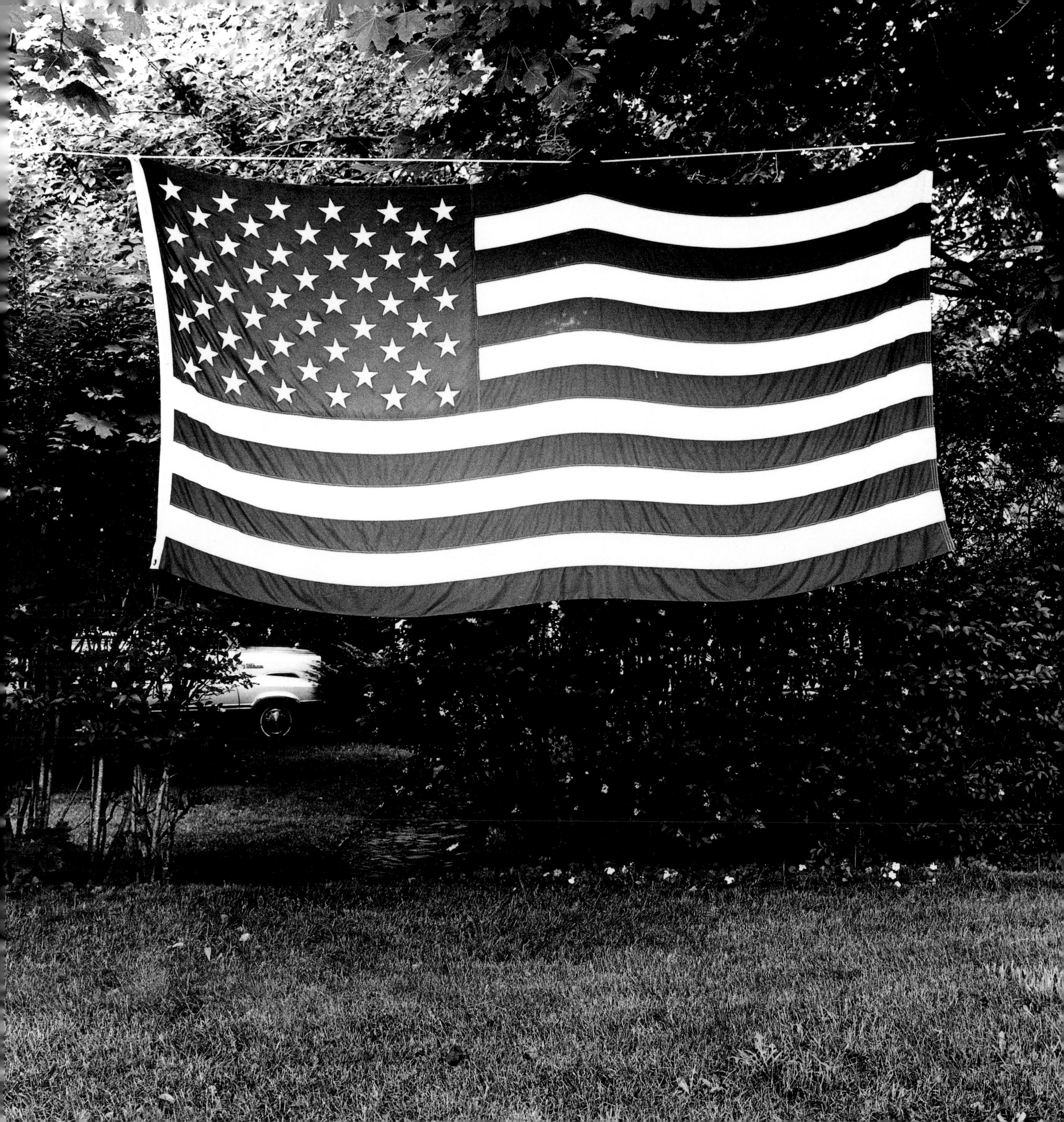

Death-row inmate in the prison in Huntsville,
Texas, **1995**

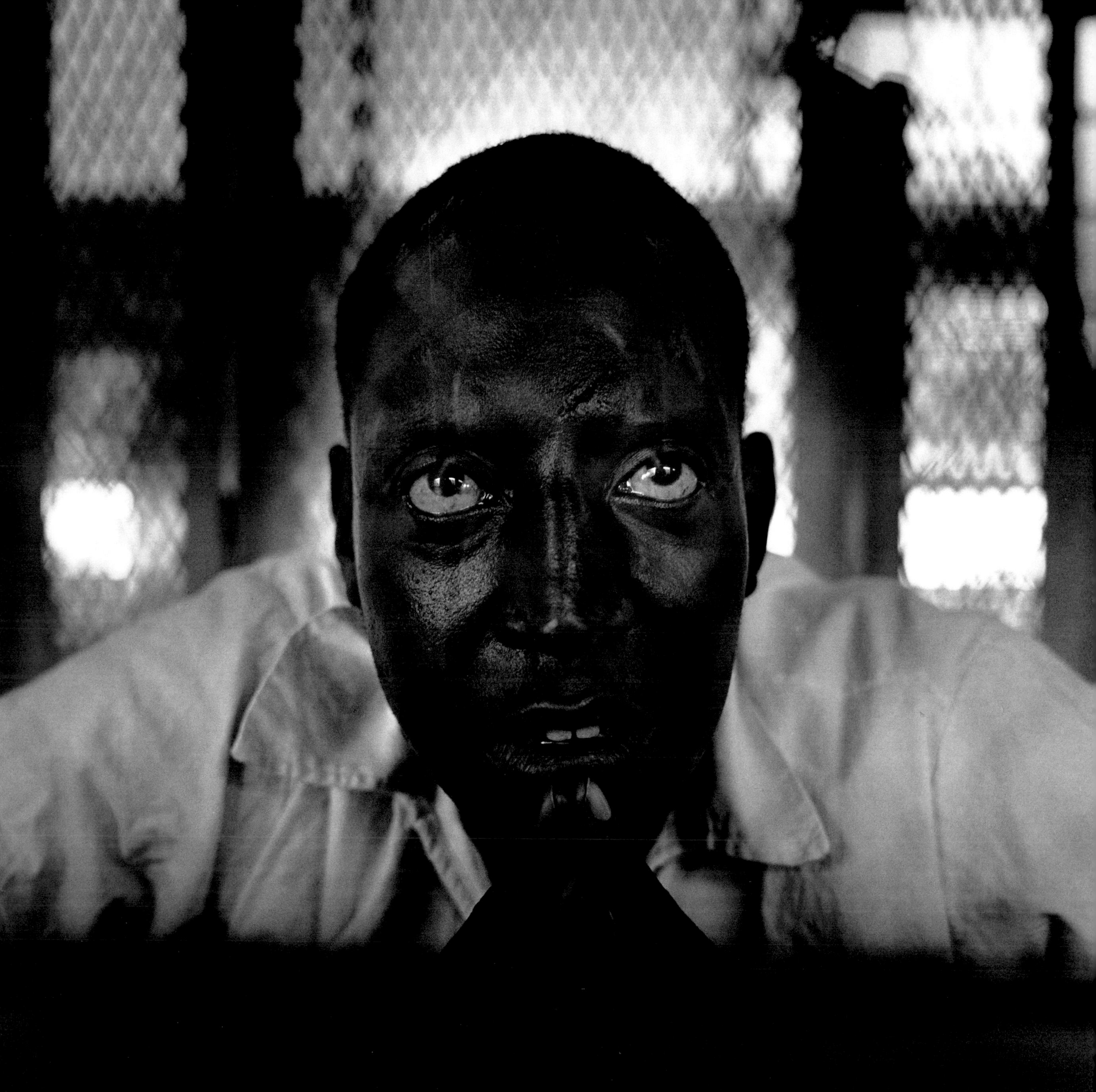

The bed on which candidates for execution
are given a lethal injection, prison in Huntsville,
Texas, **1995**

Visitors' room in the prison, Huntsville, Texas, **1995**

AIDS quilt, Washington, D.C., **1996**

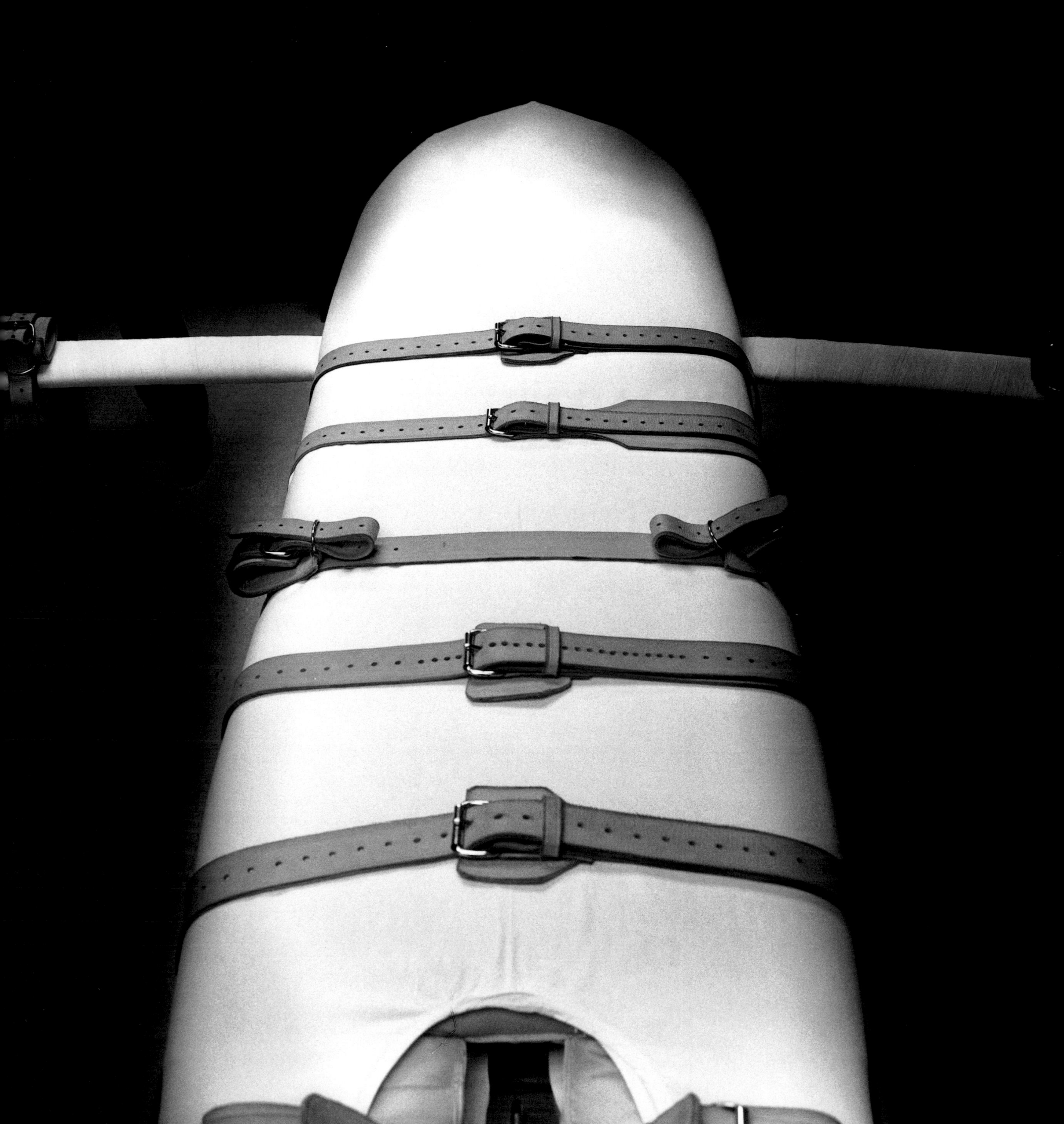

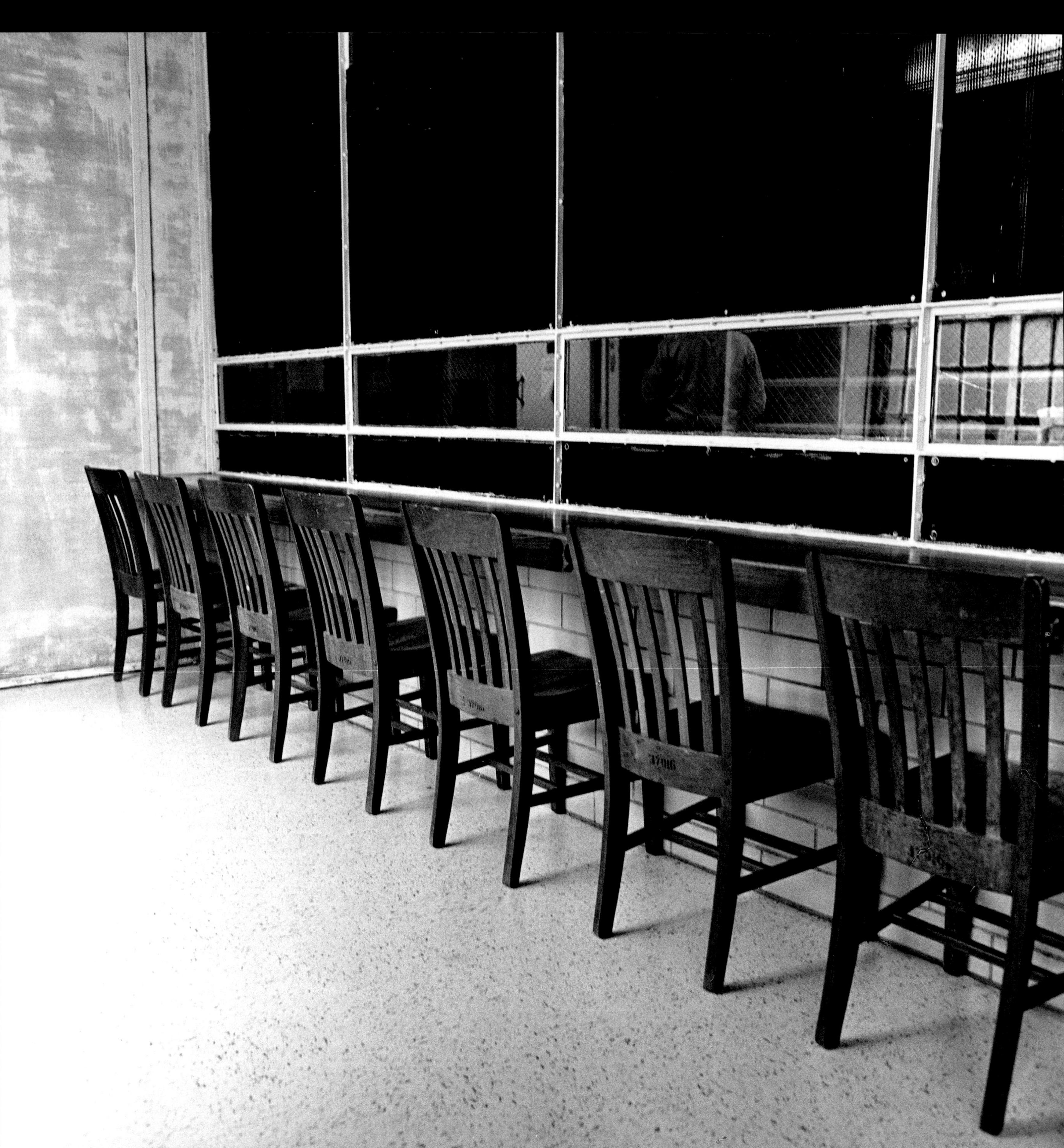

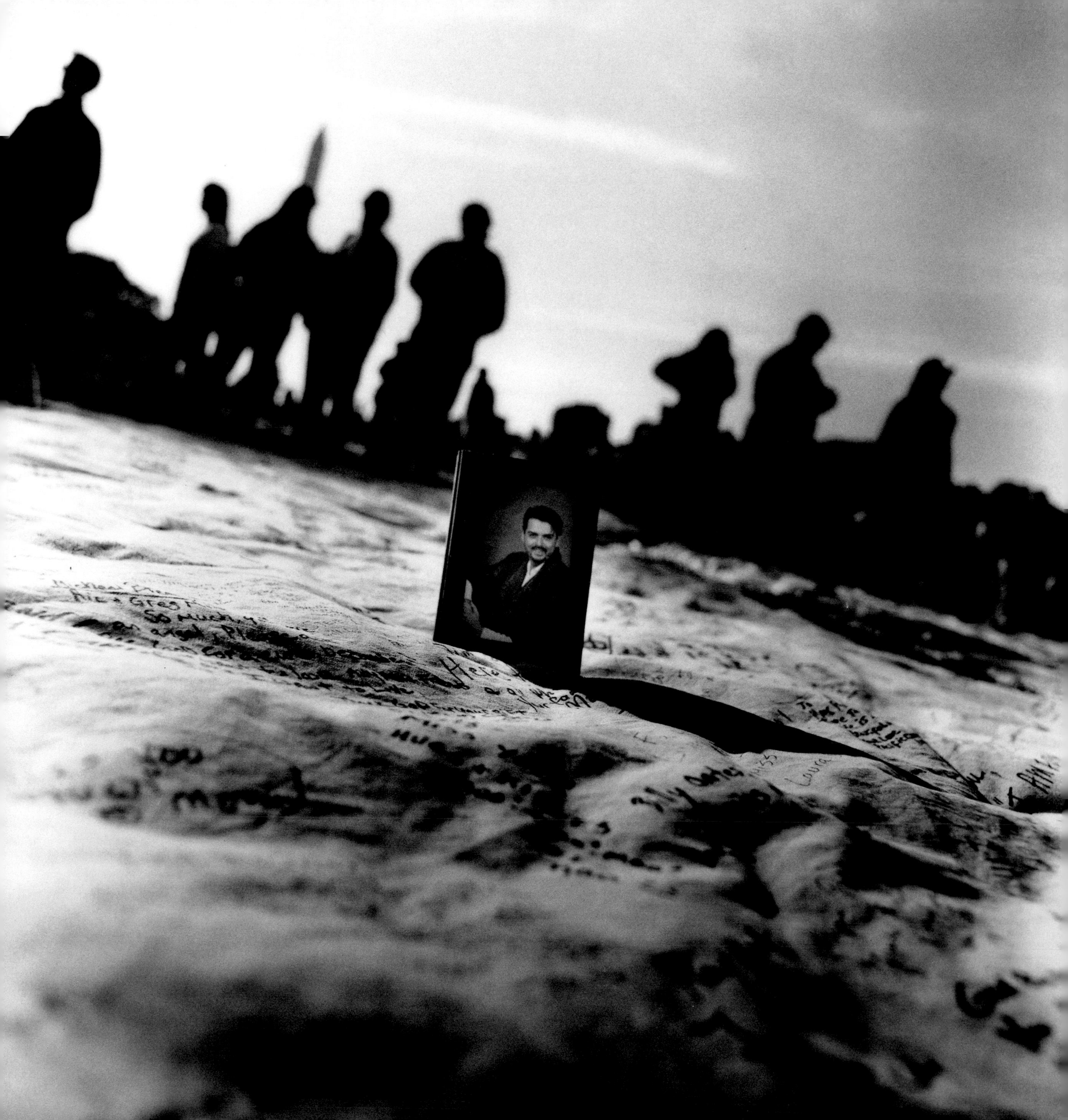

Burial of an executed convict
at the prison cemetery in Huntsville,
Texas, **1995**

Memorial wall for the murdered Hispanic singer Selena,
Houston Street, New York City, **1996**

A girl, whose boyfriend was shot to death,
Coney Island, New York, **1995**

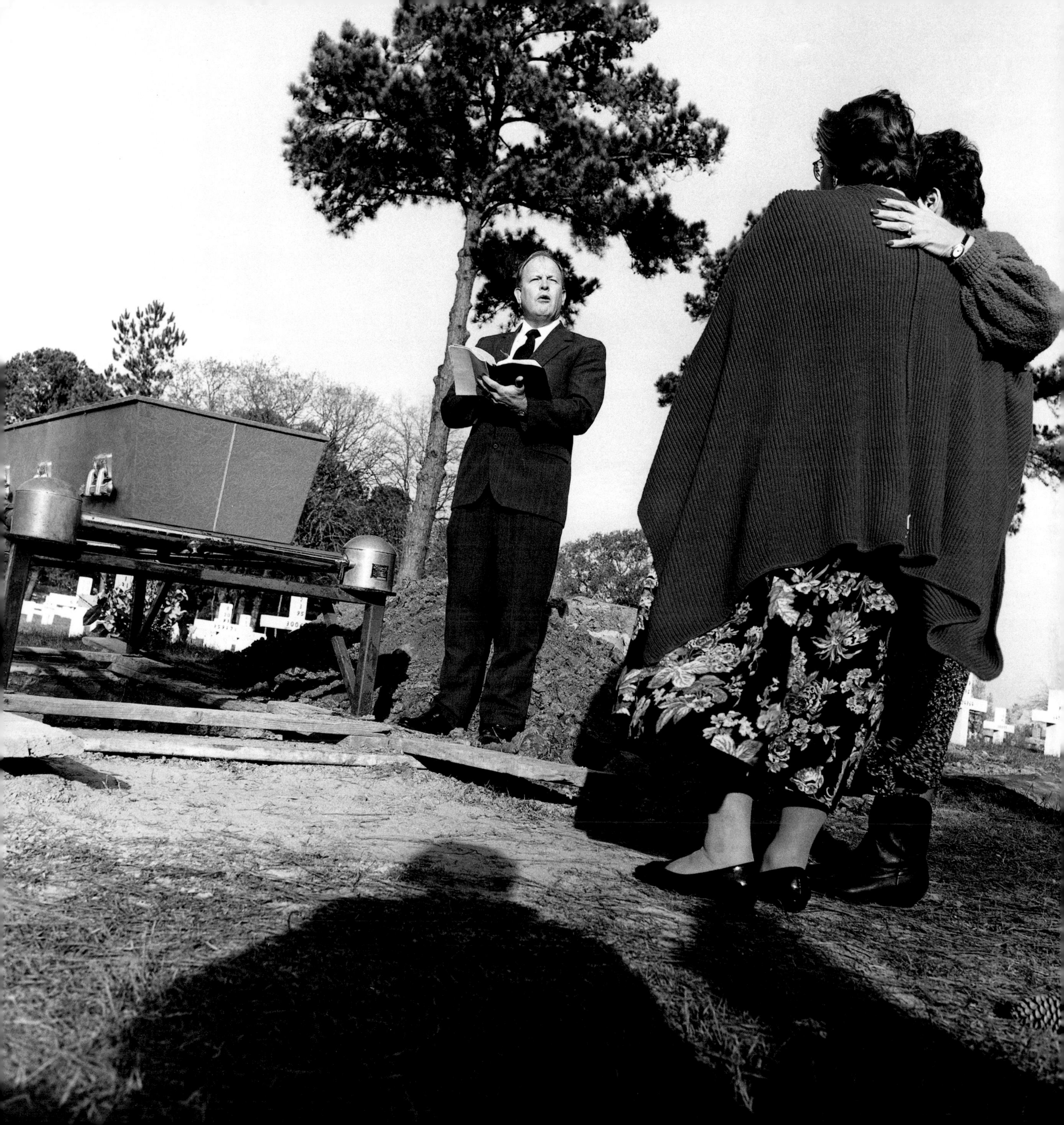

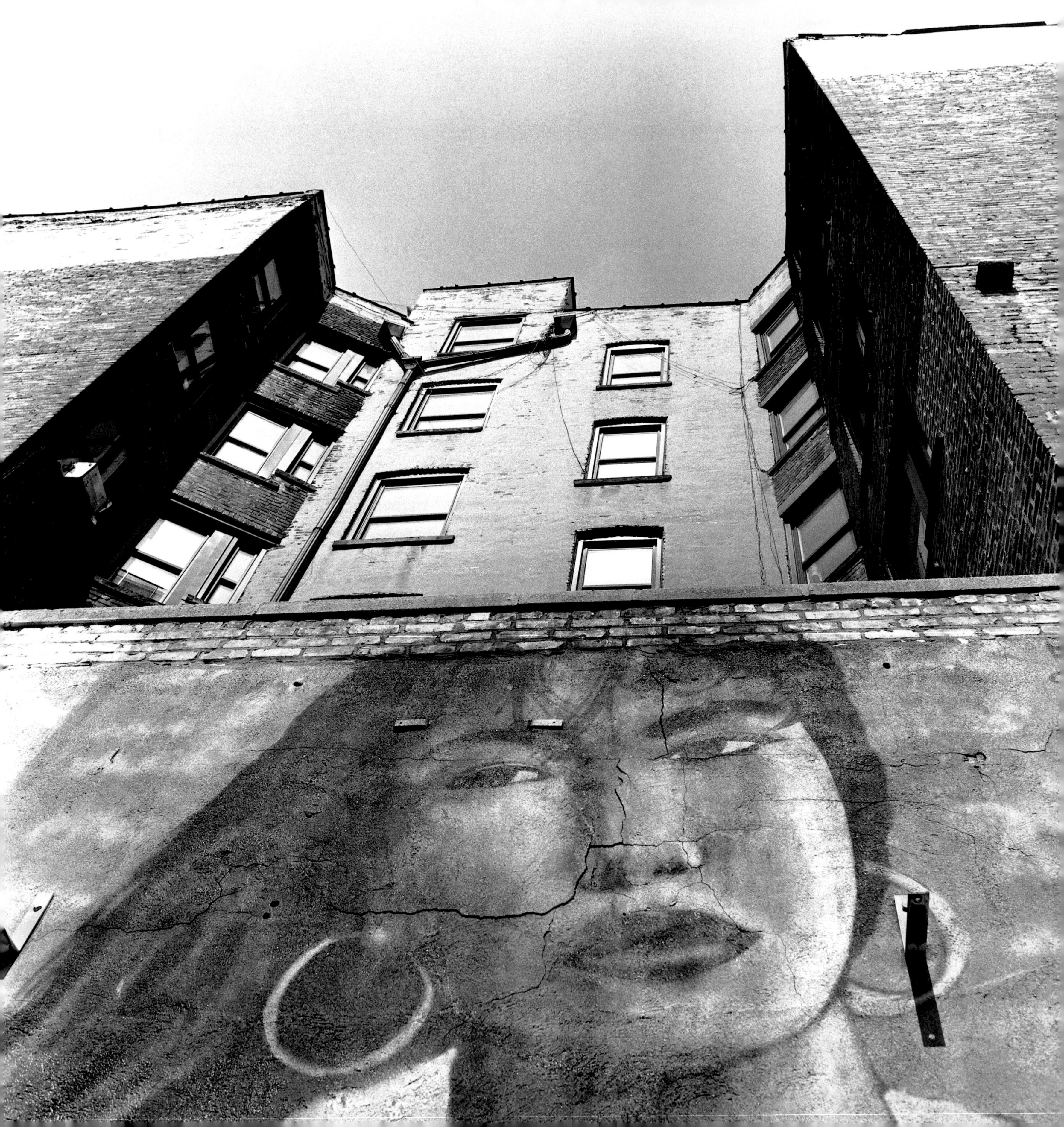

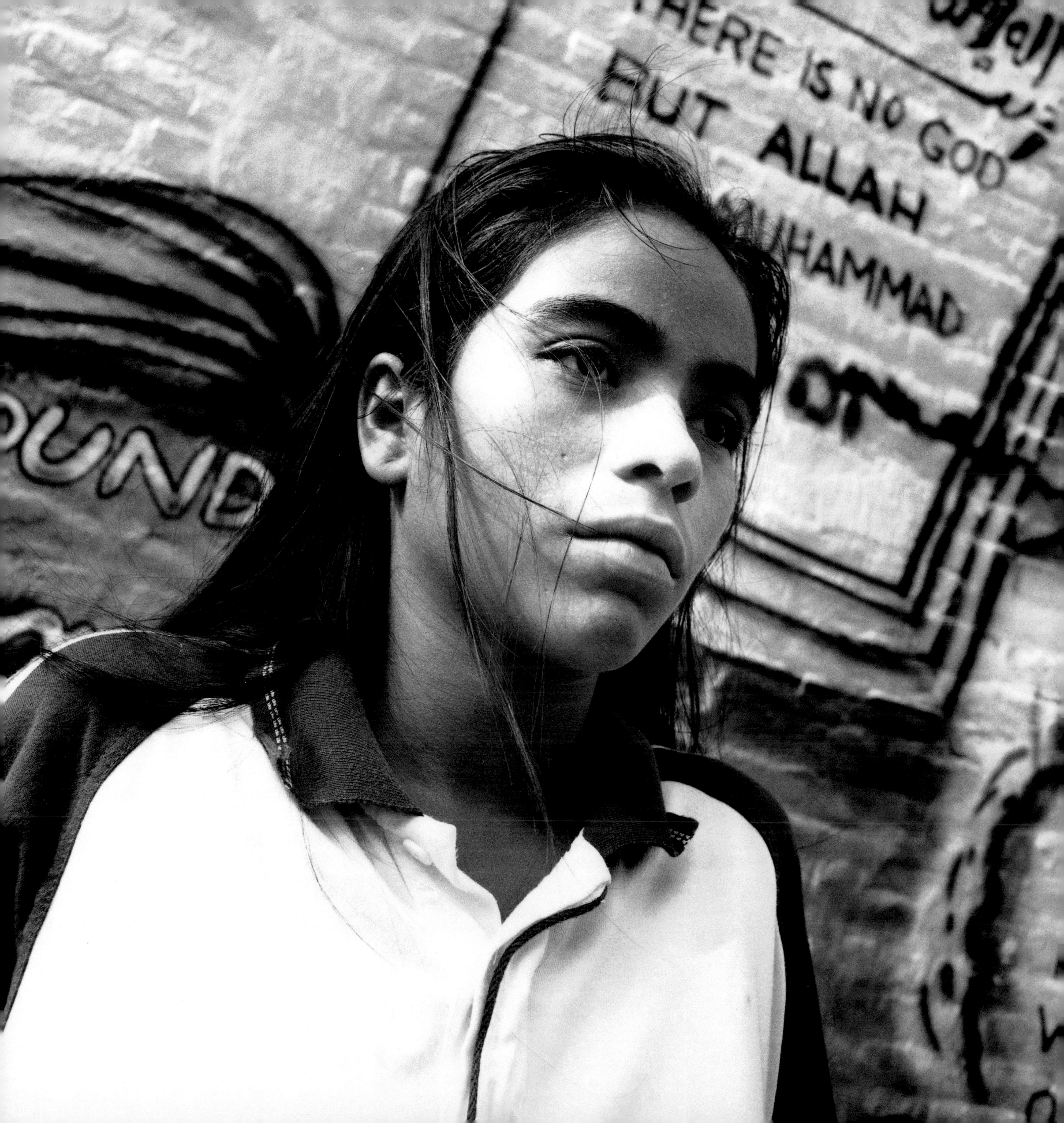
HERE IS NO GOD
ALLAH
HAMMAD

Funeral, Coney Island,
New York, **1995**

Funeral for a basketball star,
Coney Island, New York, **1995**

Gospel singers at a funeral for a basketball star,
Coney Island, New York, **1995**

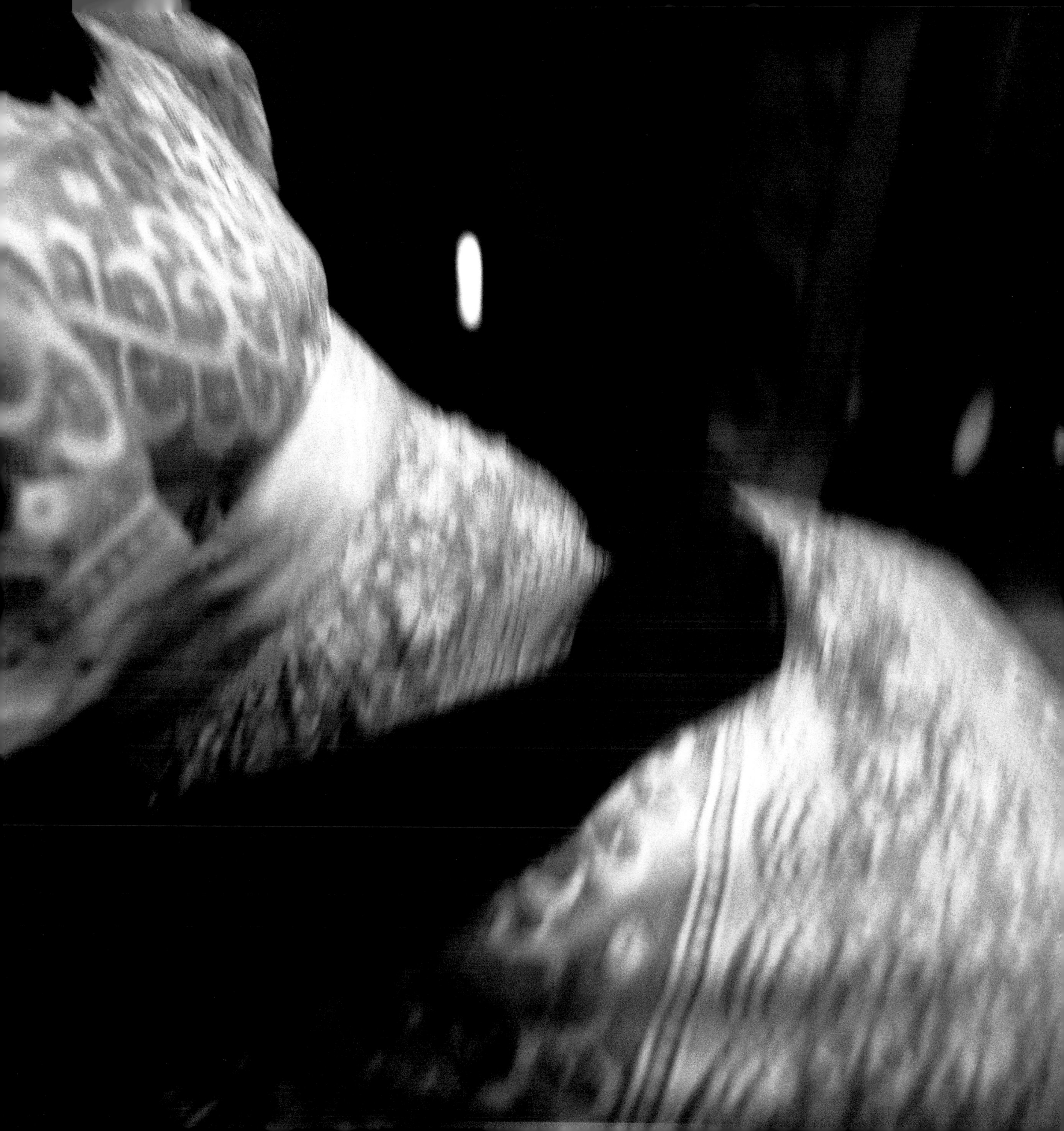

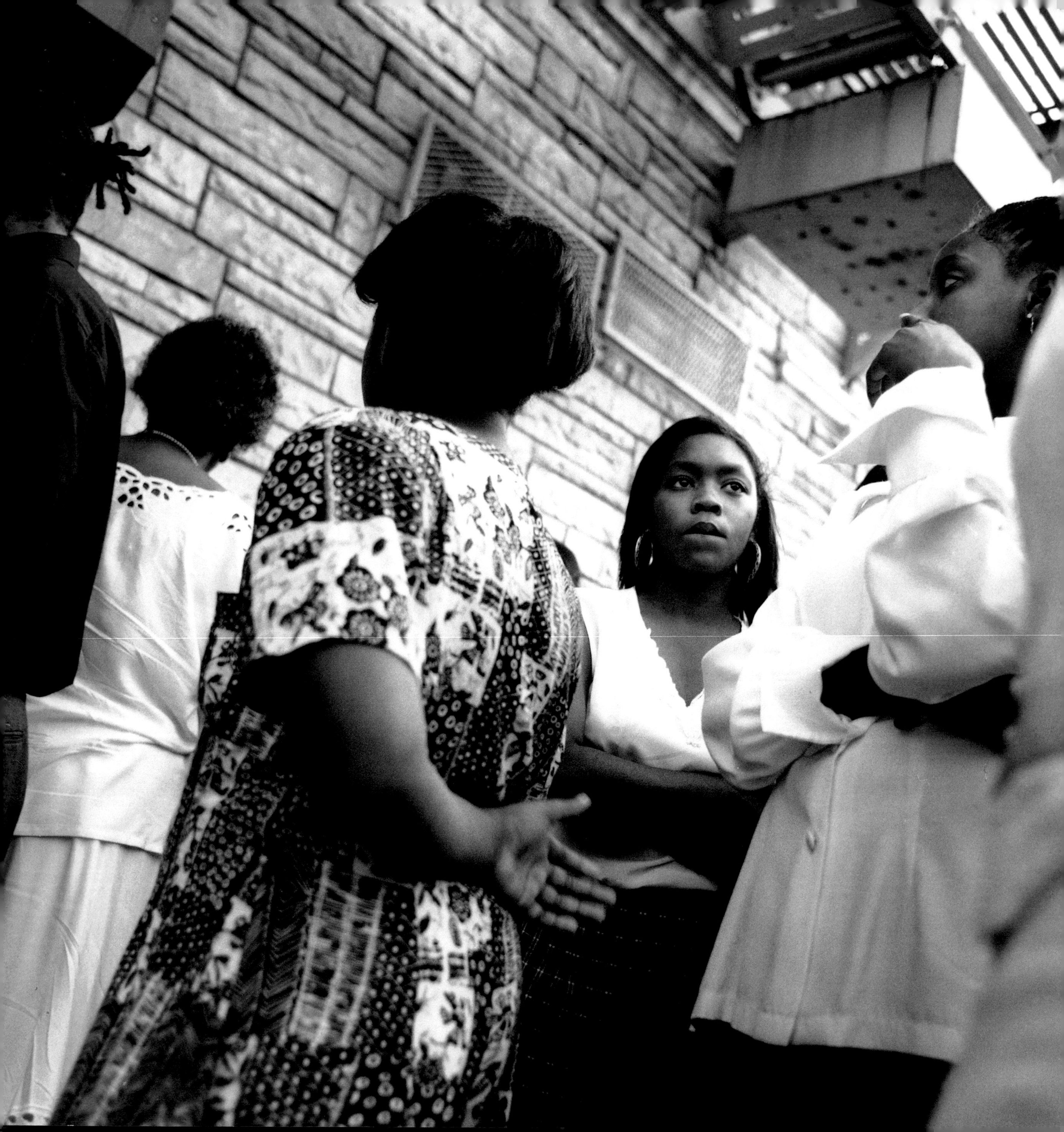

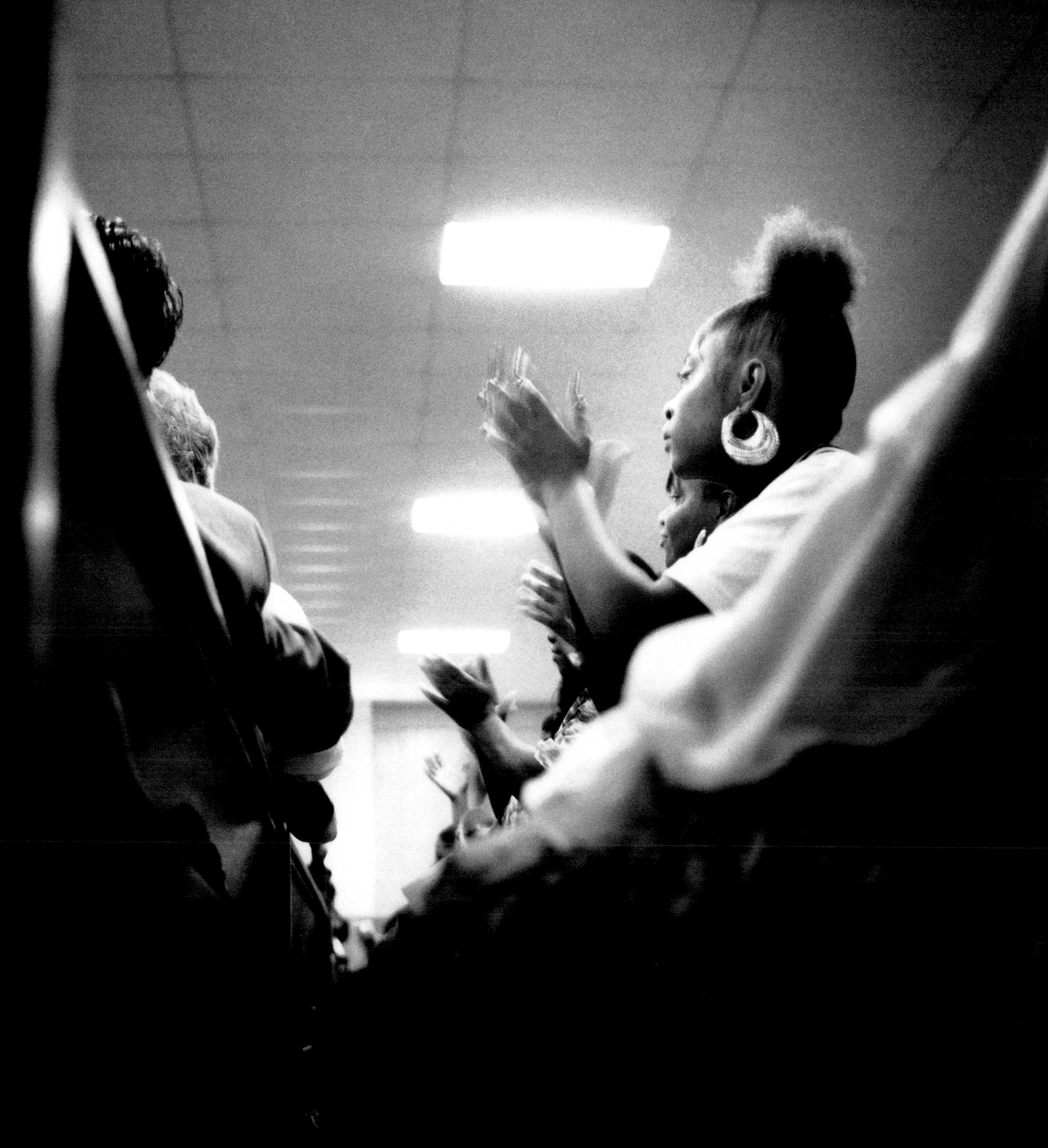

Religious rites commemorating slaves who died.
Coney Island, New York, **1995**

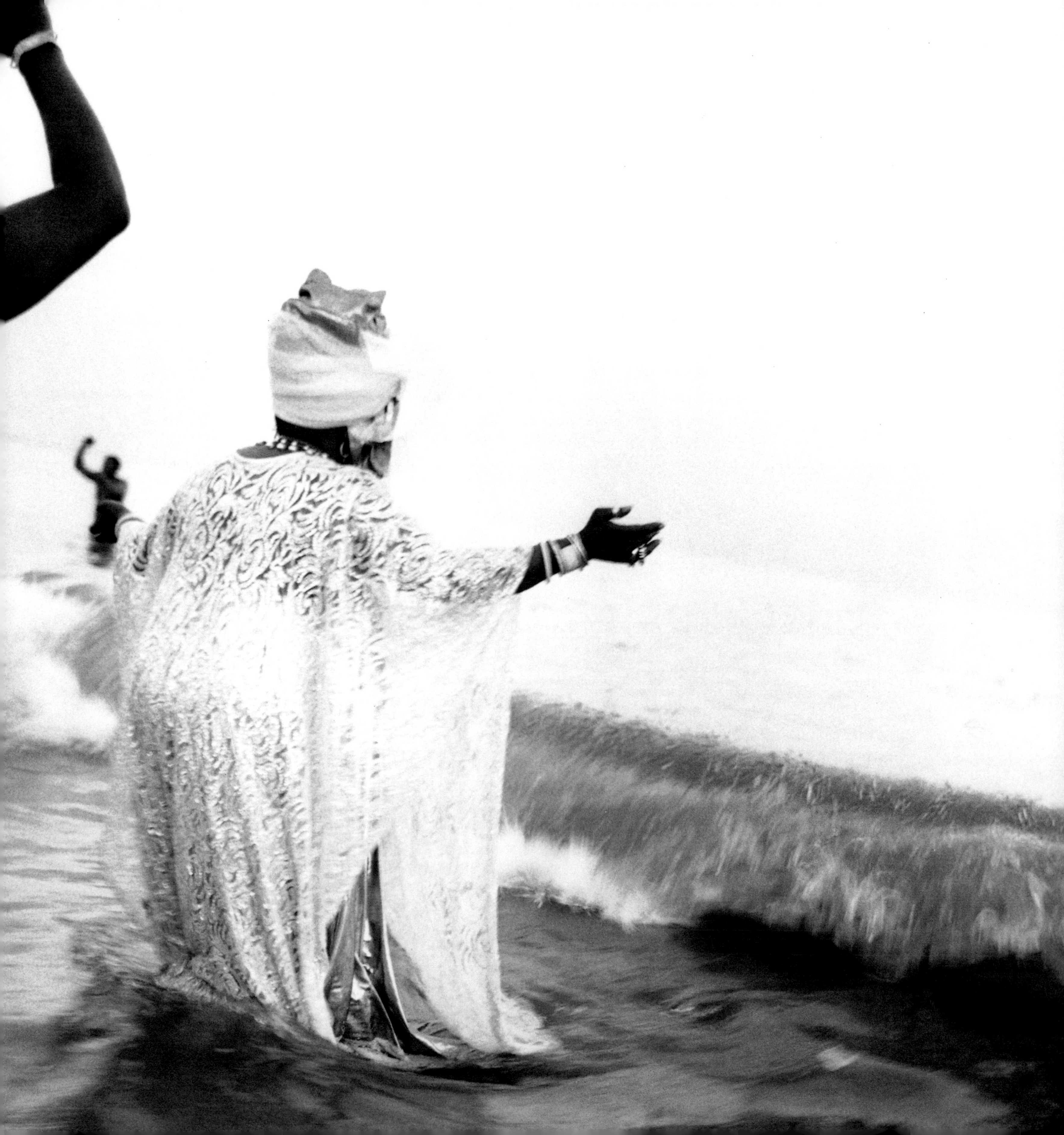

IV.

Tourist in Monument Valley, Arizona, **1995**

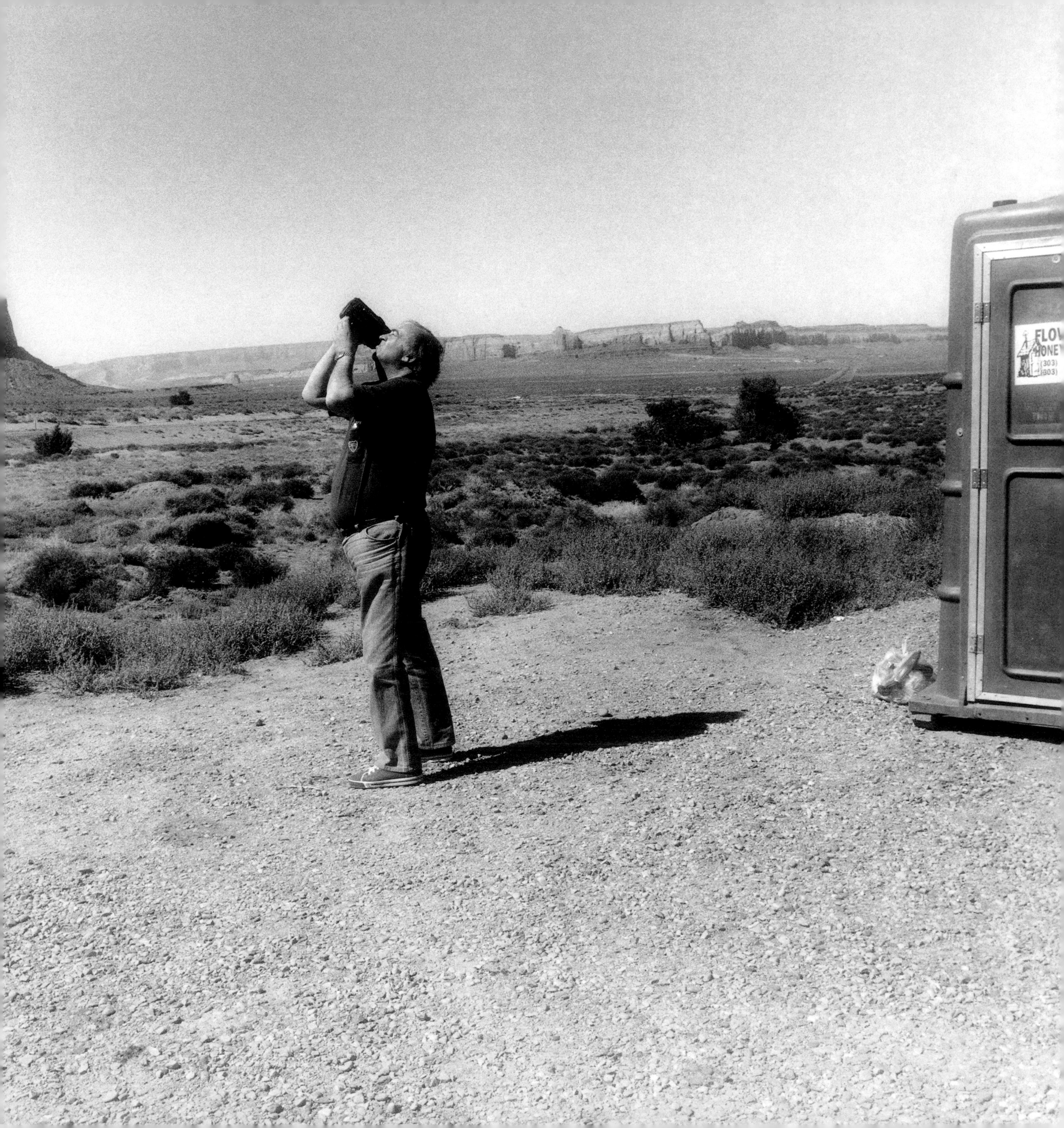
FLO
HONE
(303)
(303)

The Wigwam Motel, New Mexico. **1995**

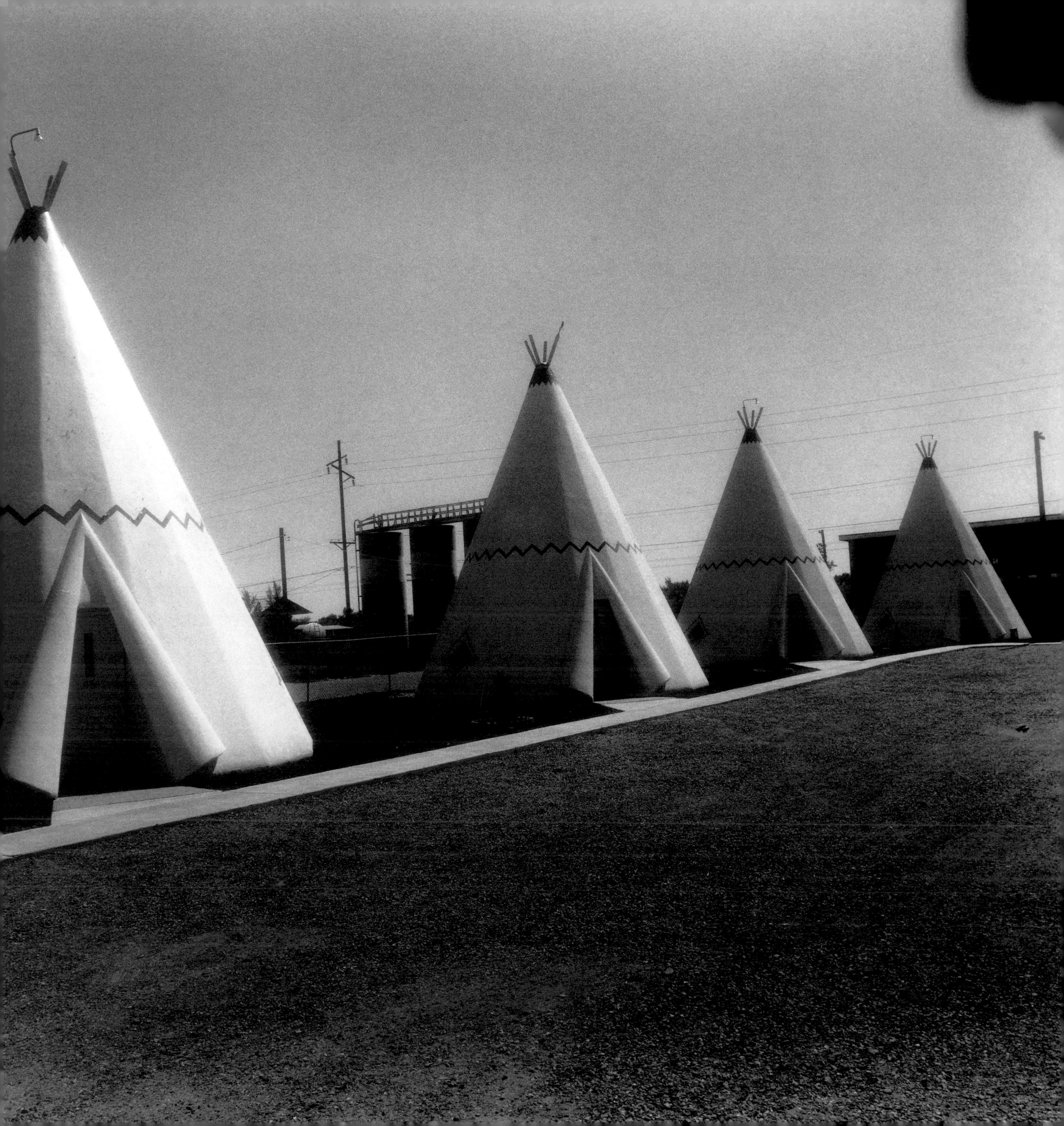

Tourists in Monument Valley, Arizona, **1995**

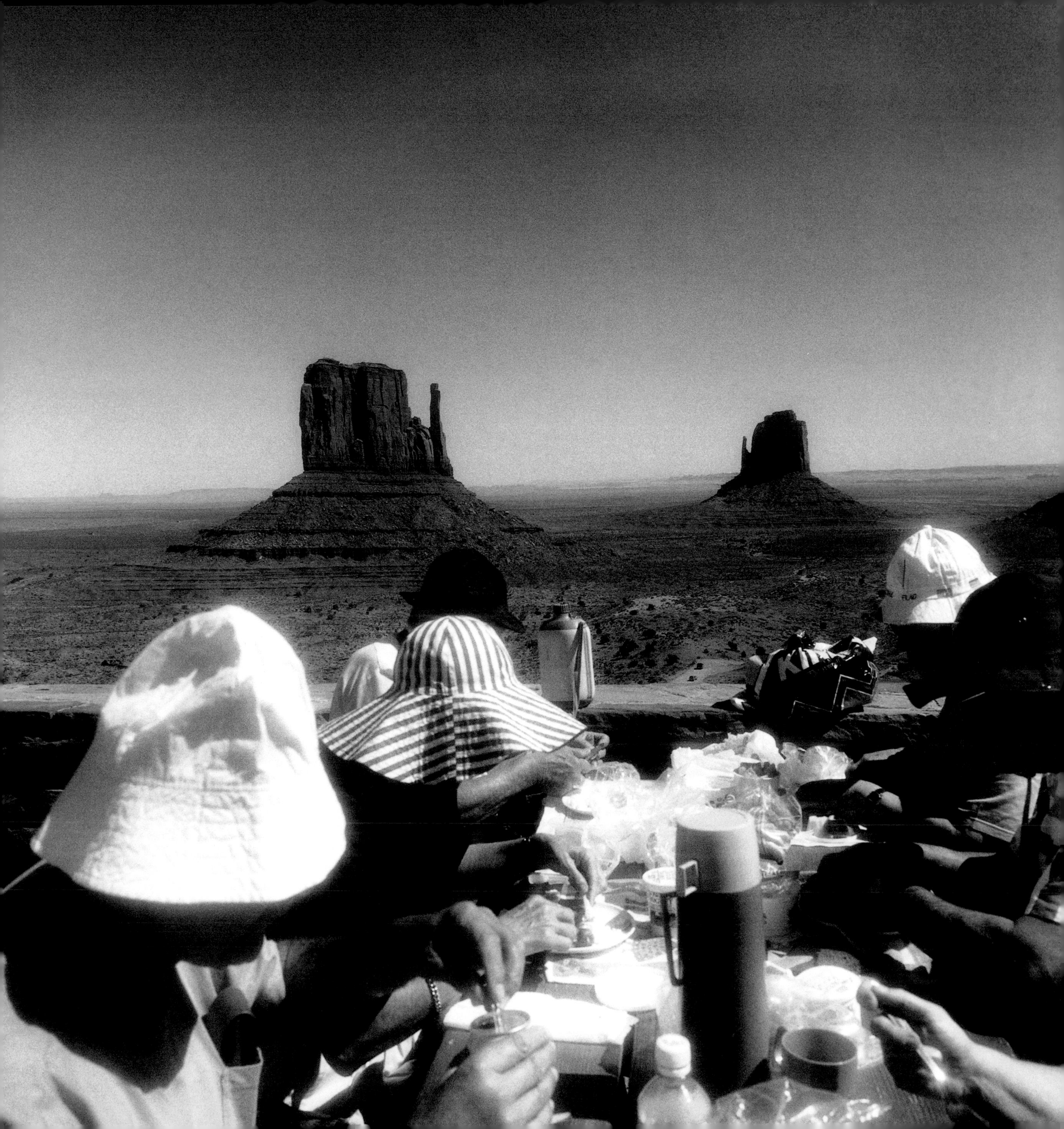

A cowboy on a Greyhound bus, Reno, Nevada, **1995**

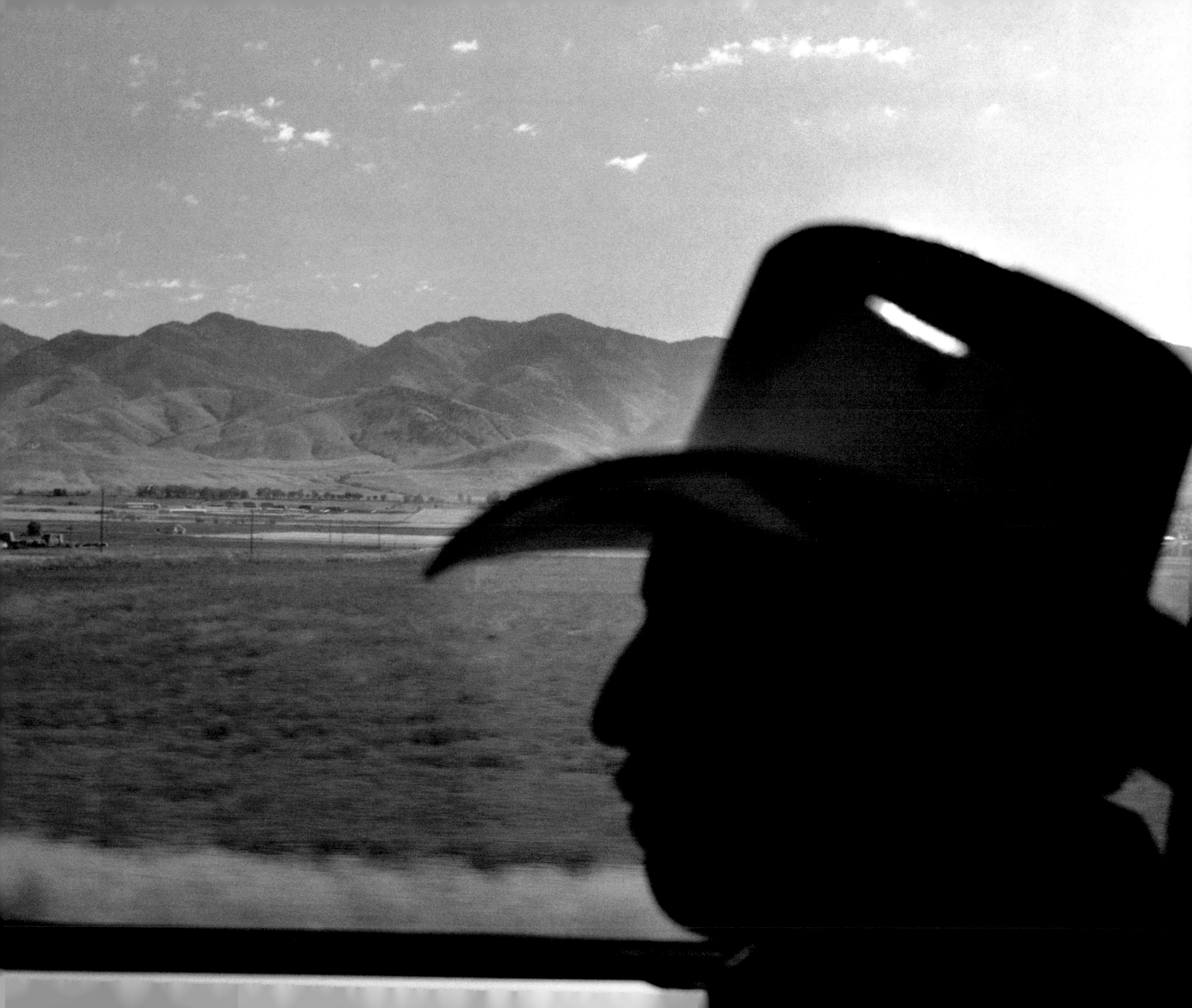

A traveler on a Greyhound bus,
Reno, Nevada, **1995**

Nevada landscape, **1995**

A cowboy in a laundromat in Gallup,
New Mexico, **1995**

A young rodeo cowboy at the Navajo Rodeo,
Fort Defiance, Arizona, **1997**

Singing the National Anthem at the
start of the Navajo Rodeo, Fort Defiance,
Arizona, **1997**

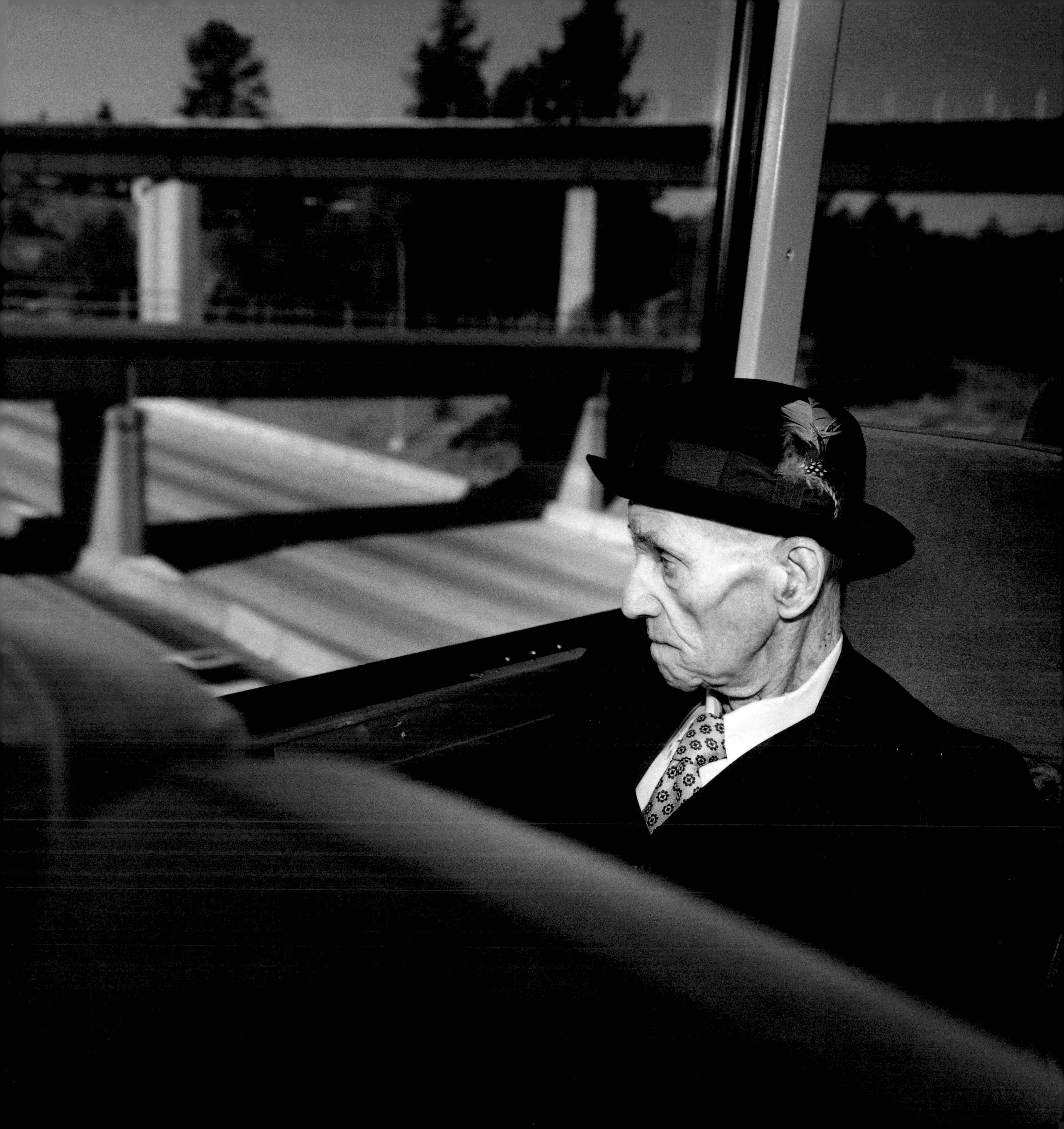

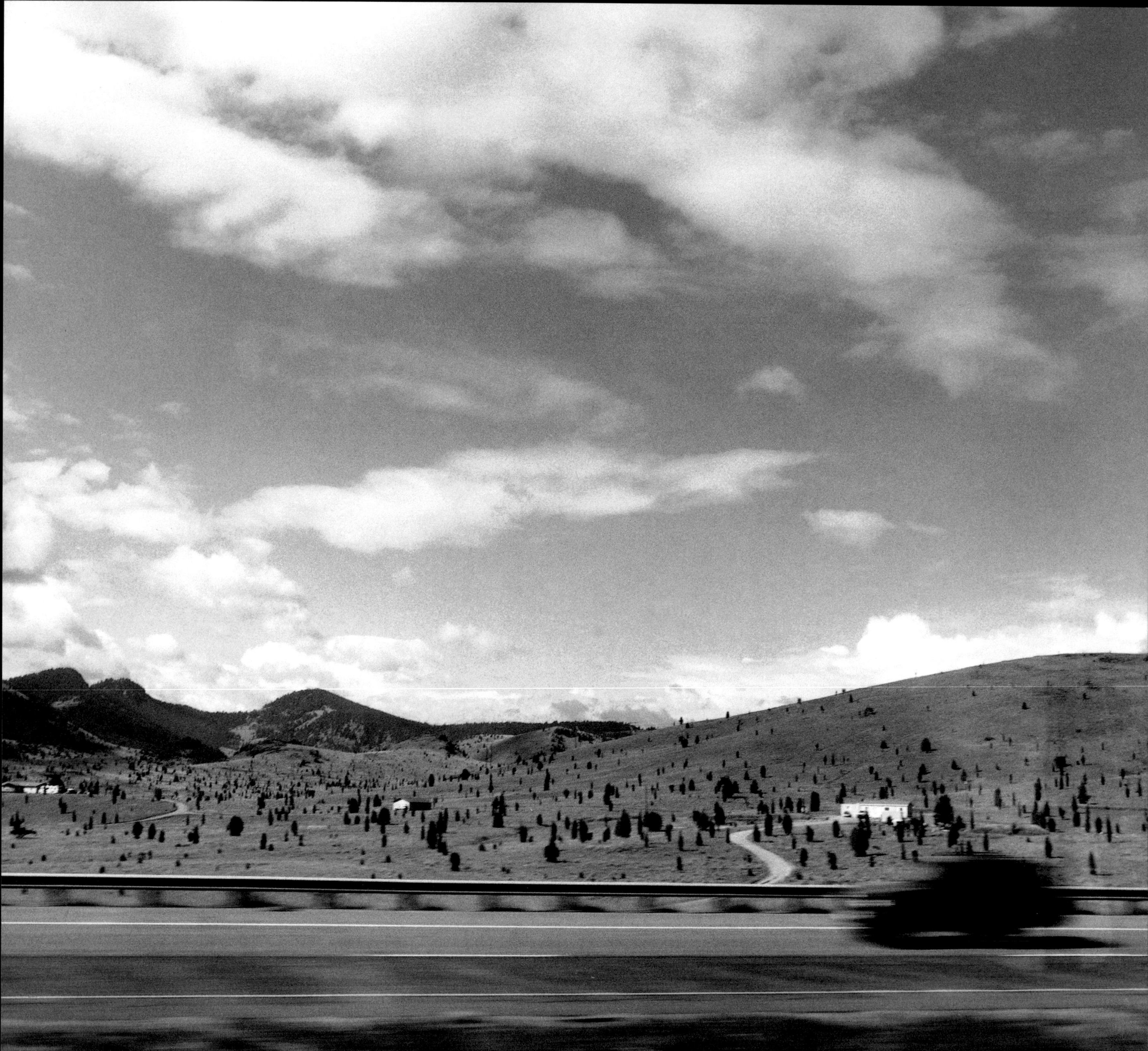

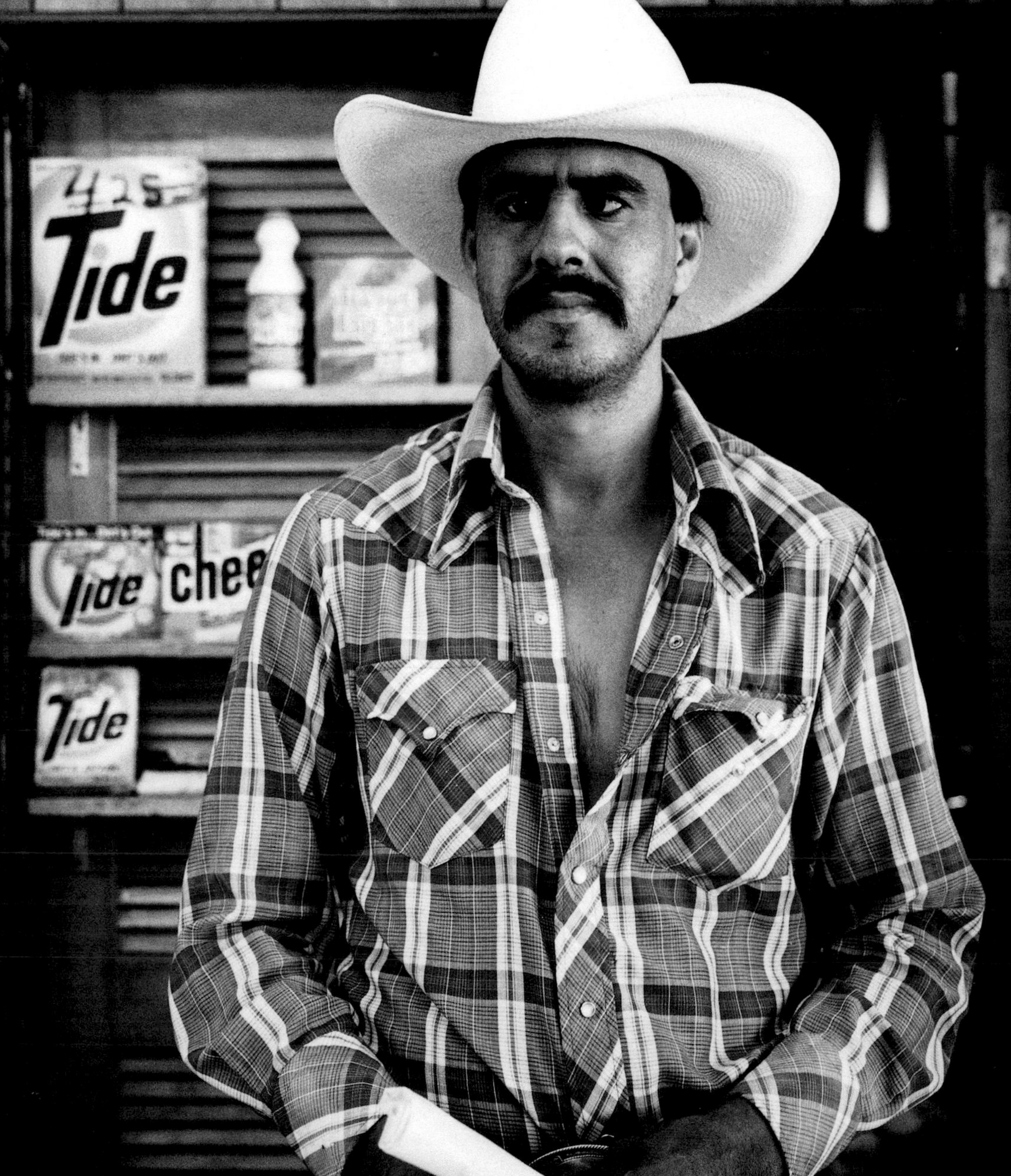
CHANGE
Tide
Tide
Tide

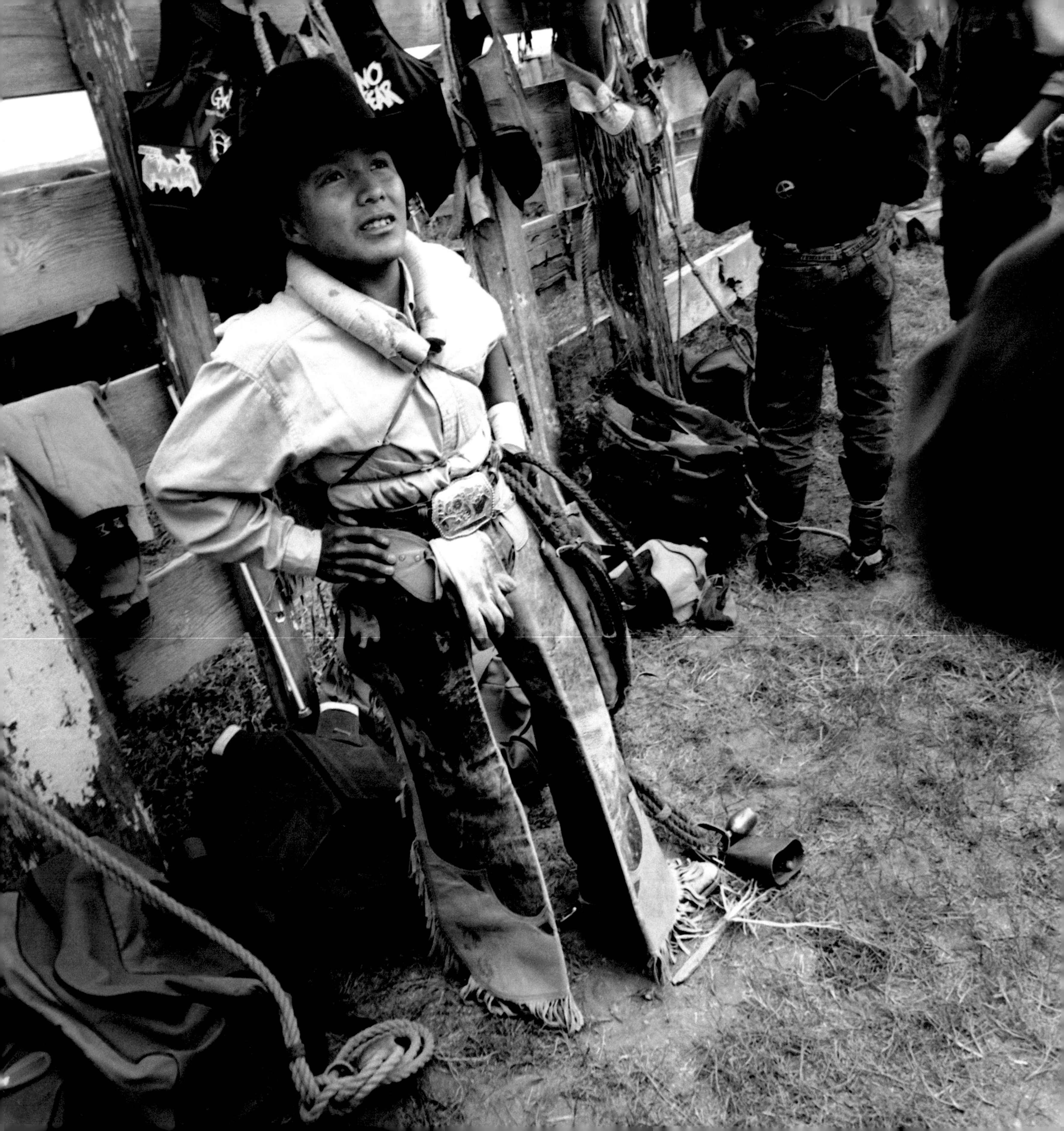

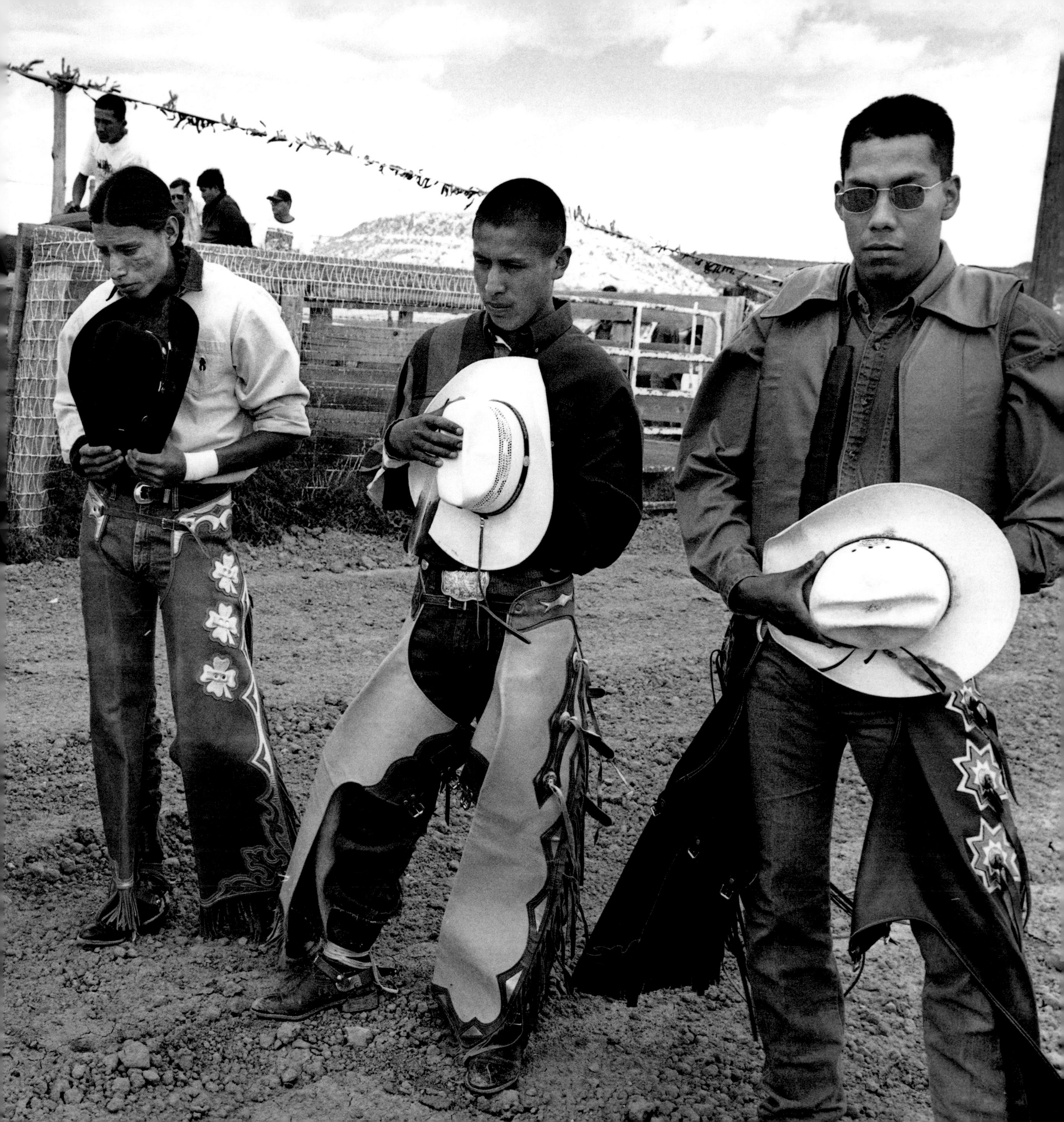

Guns laid to rest after a pheasant hunt,
Pawling, New York, **1996**

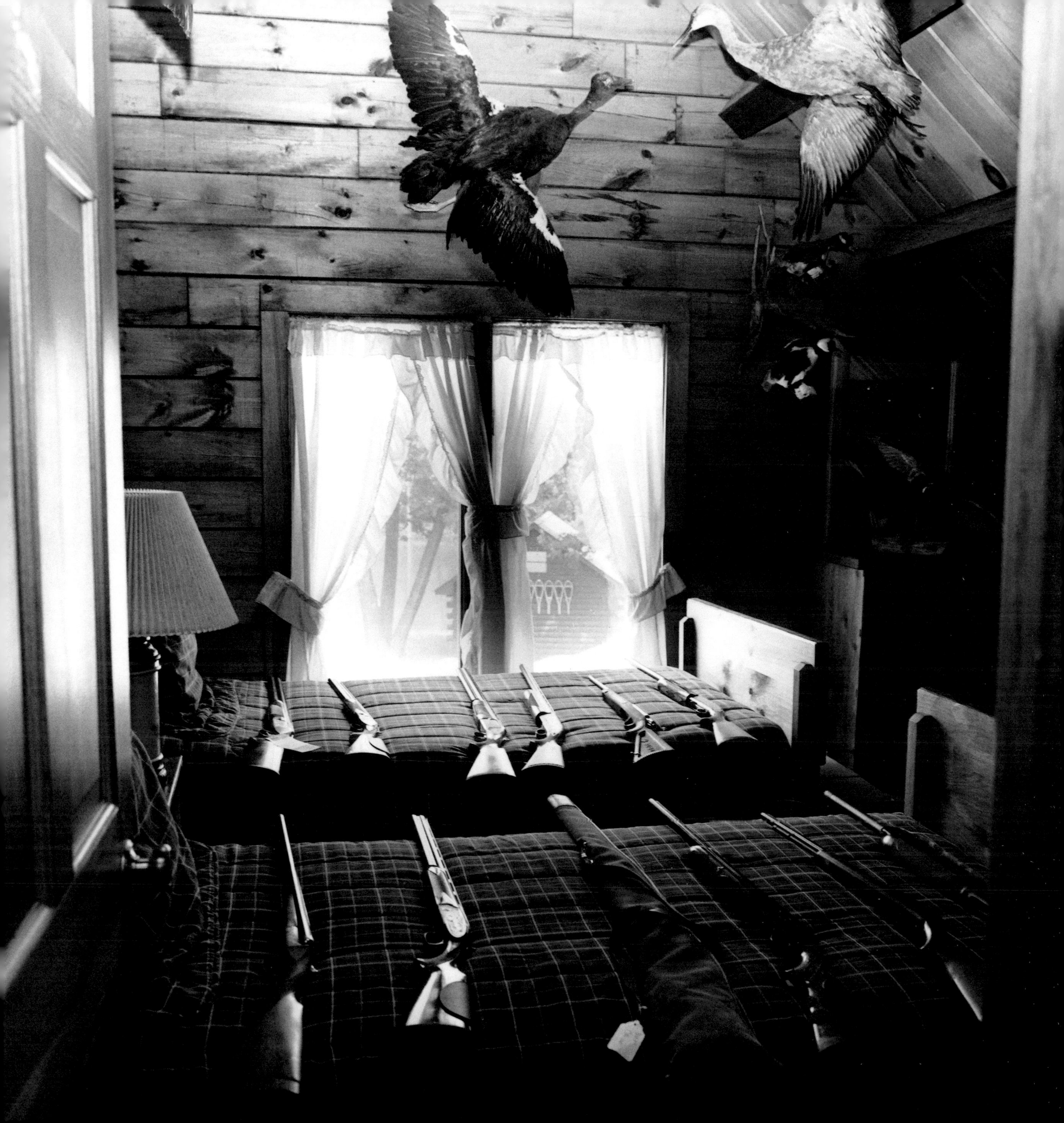

Fourteen-year-old girl marksmen from
California with high-powered rifles, Camp Perry competition,
Cleveland, Ohio, **1994**

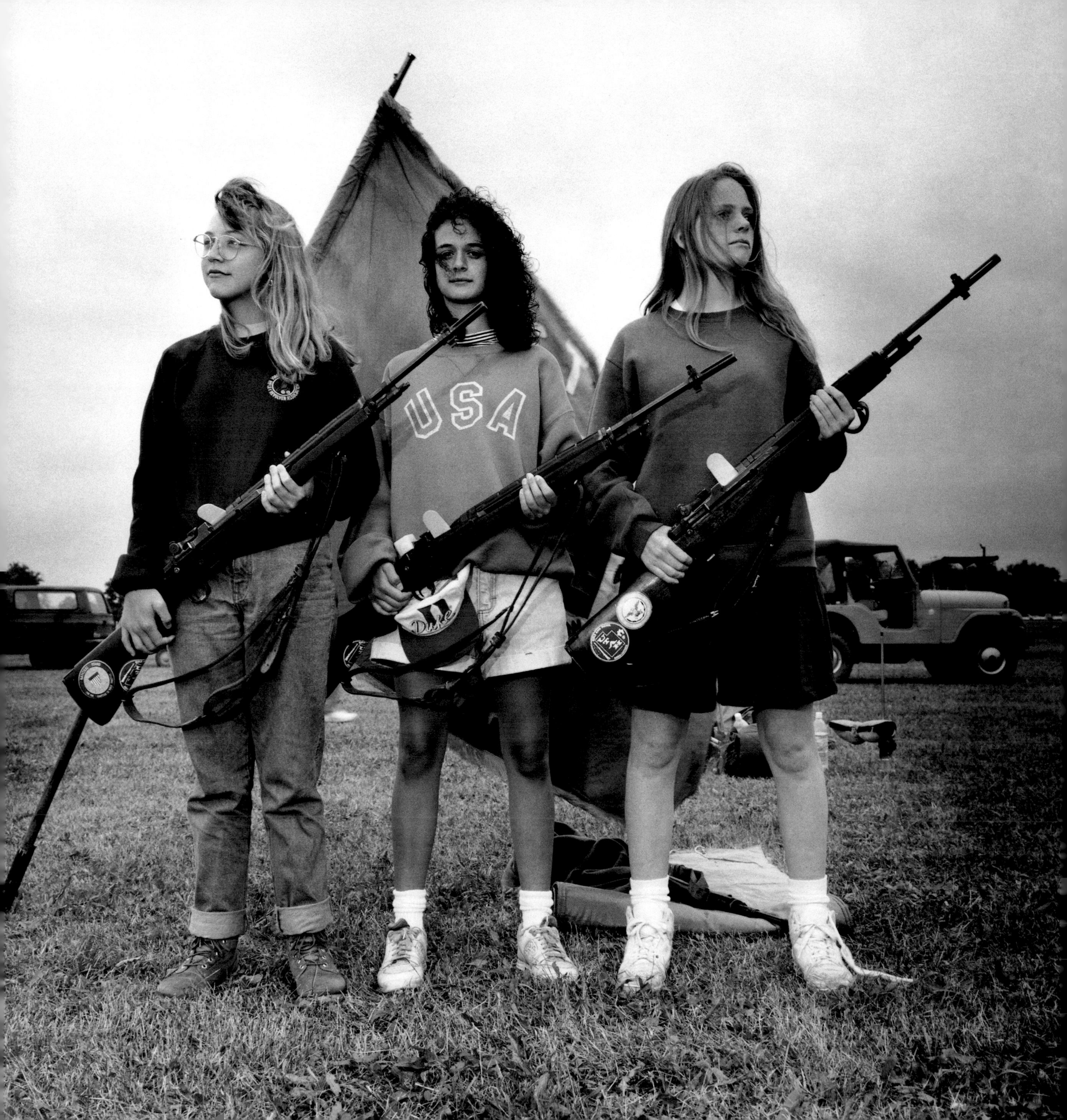
USA
Duke

Employee at a gun shop, New York City, **1993**

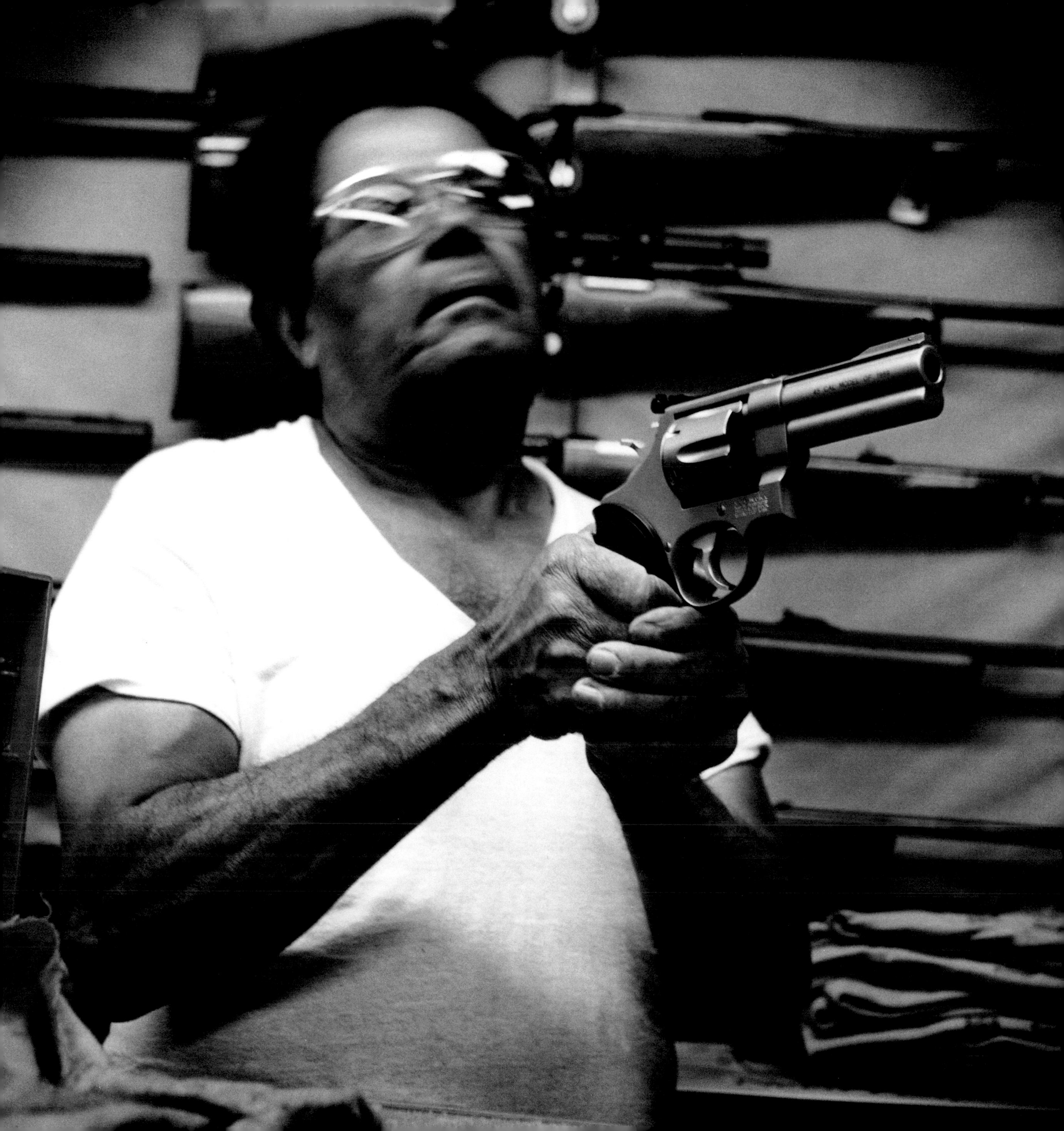

Vietnam veterans at a parade
for the carriers of the Olympic flame,
Cheyenne, Wyoming, **1995**

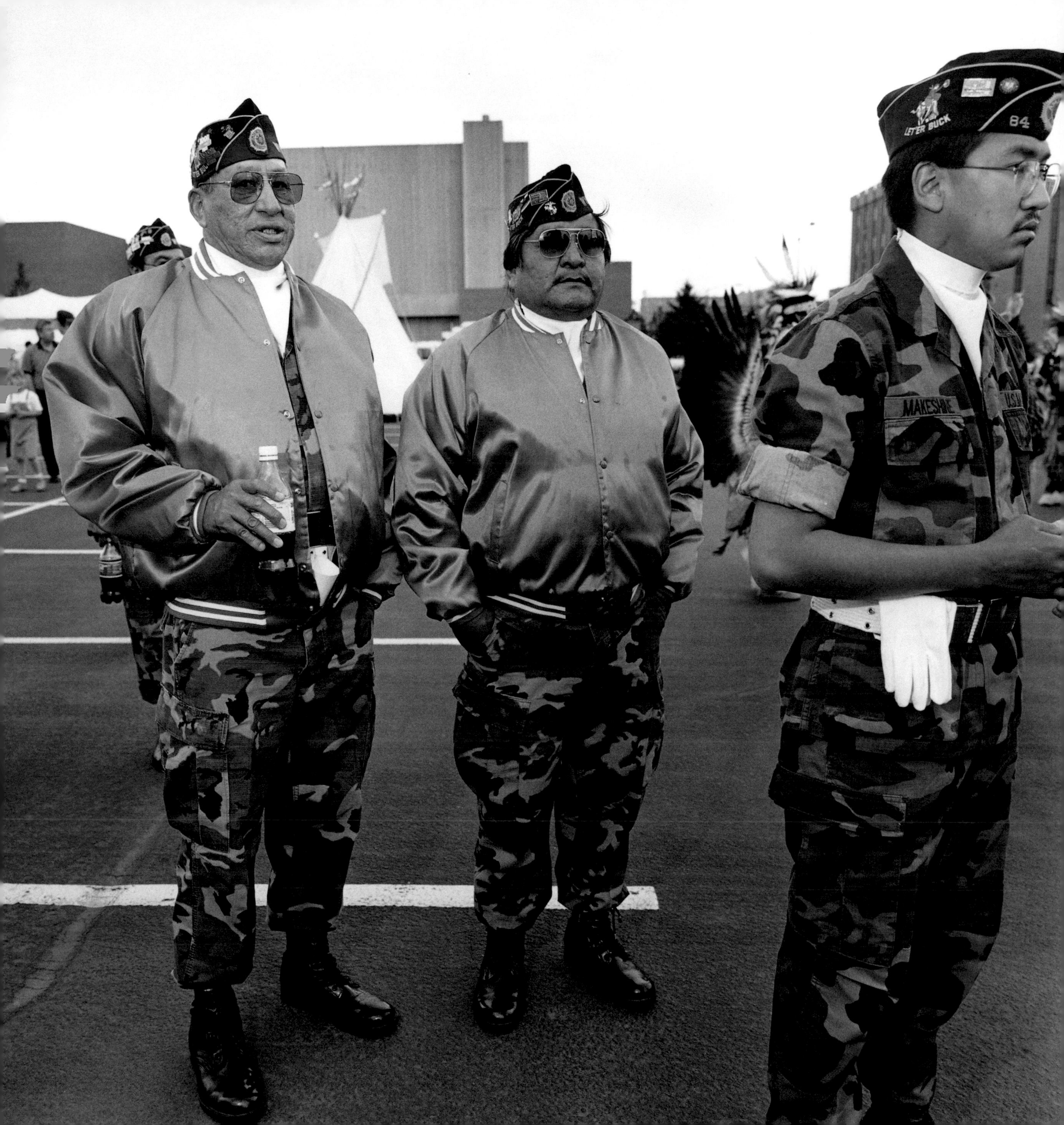

LET'ER BUCK
84
MAKESHINE

Fan at a country-and-western concert,
Branson, Missouri, **1993**

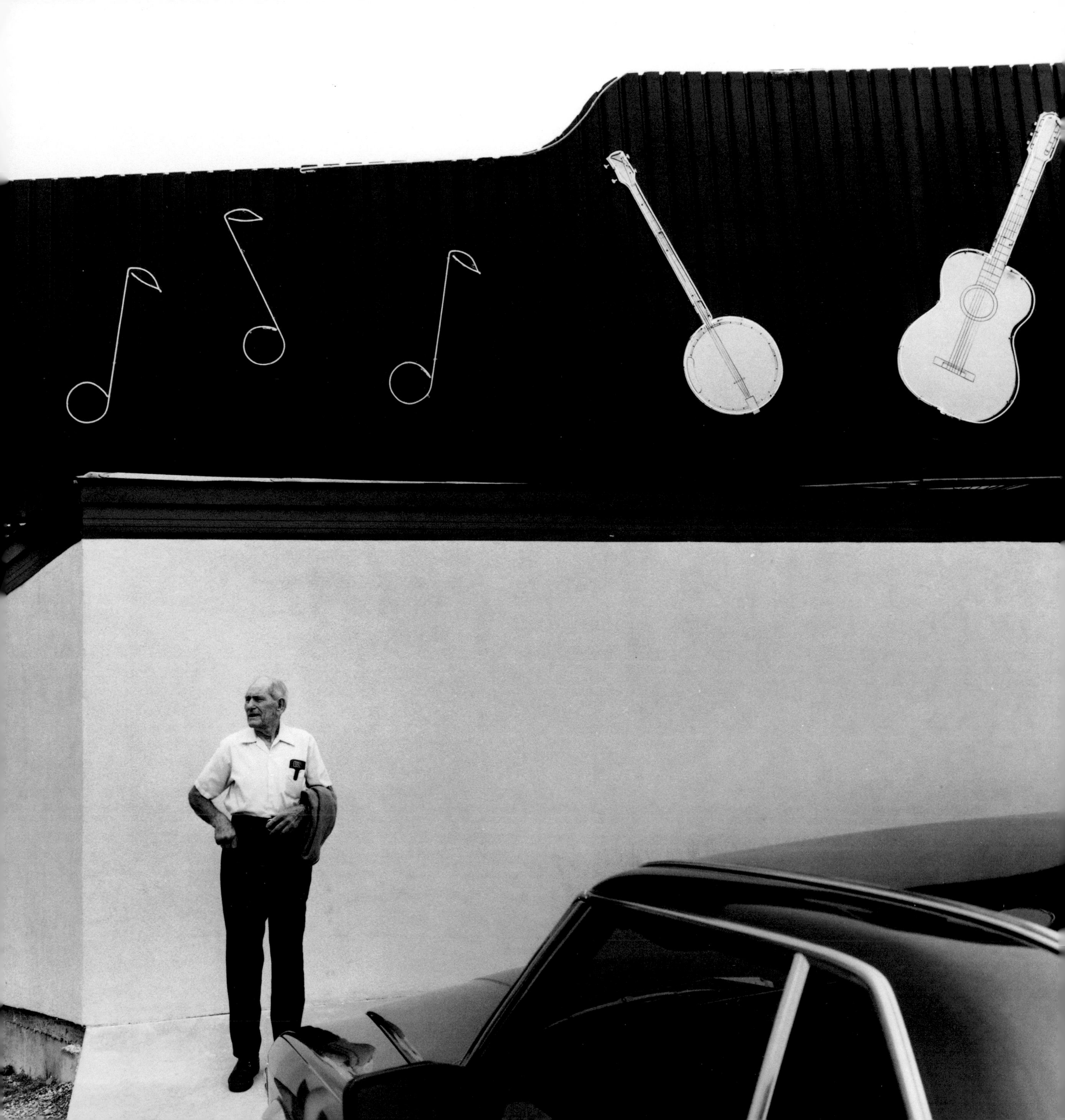

Country-and-western singer Mel Tillis,
Branson, Missouri, **1993**

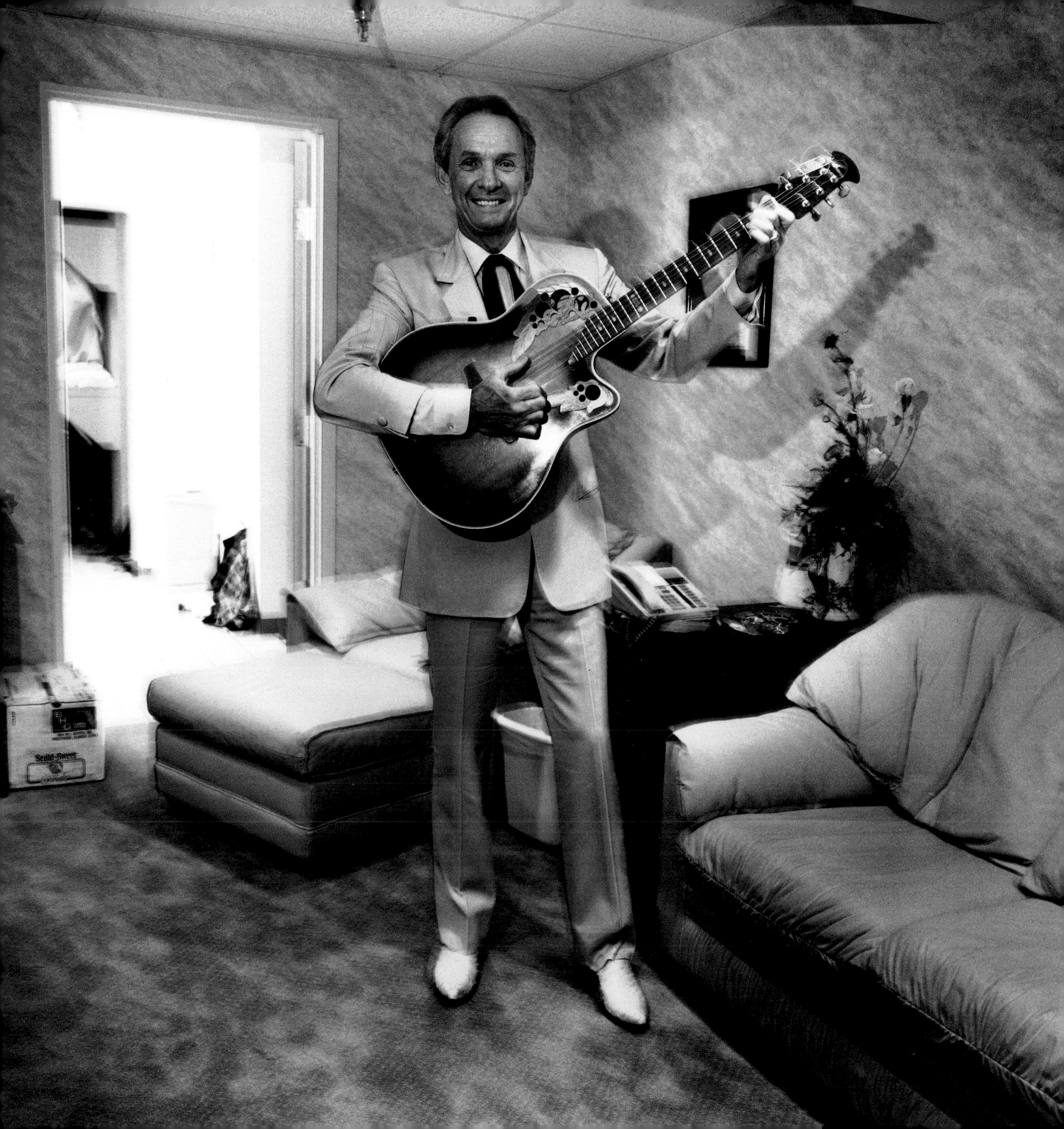
B H G
Seald-Sweet

The Moore Brothers, country-and-western talents,
Branson, Missouri, **1993**

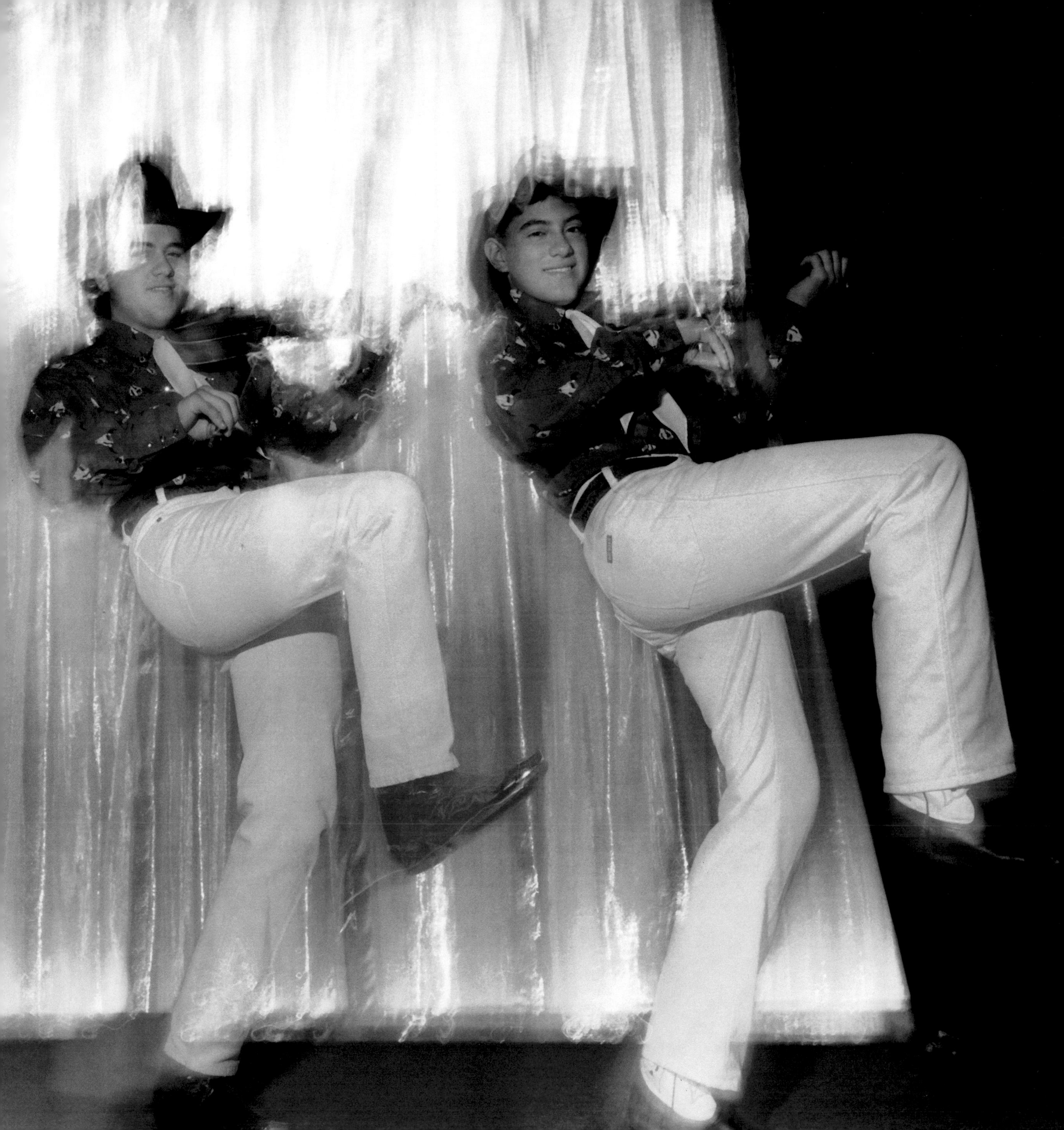

The fantastic fiddler Shoji Tabuchi saying goodbye to his fans, Branson, Missouri, **1993**

Mural, Clarksdale, Mississippi, **1995**

Announcer, Coney Island, New York, **1989**

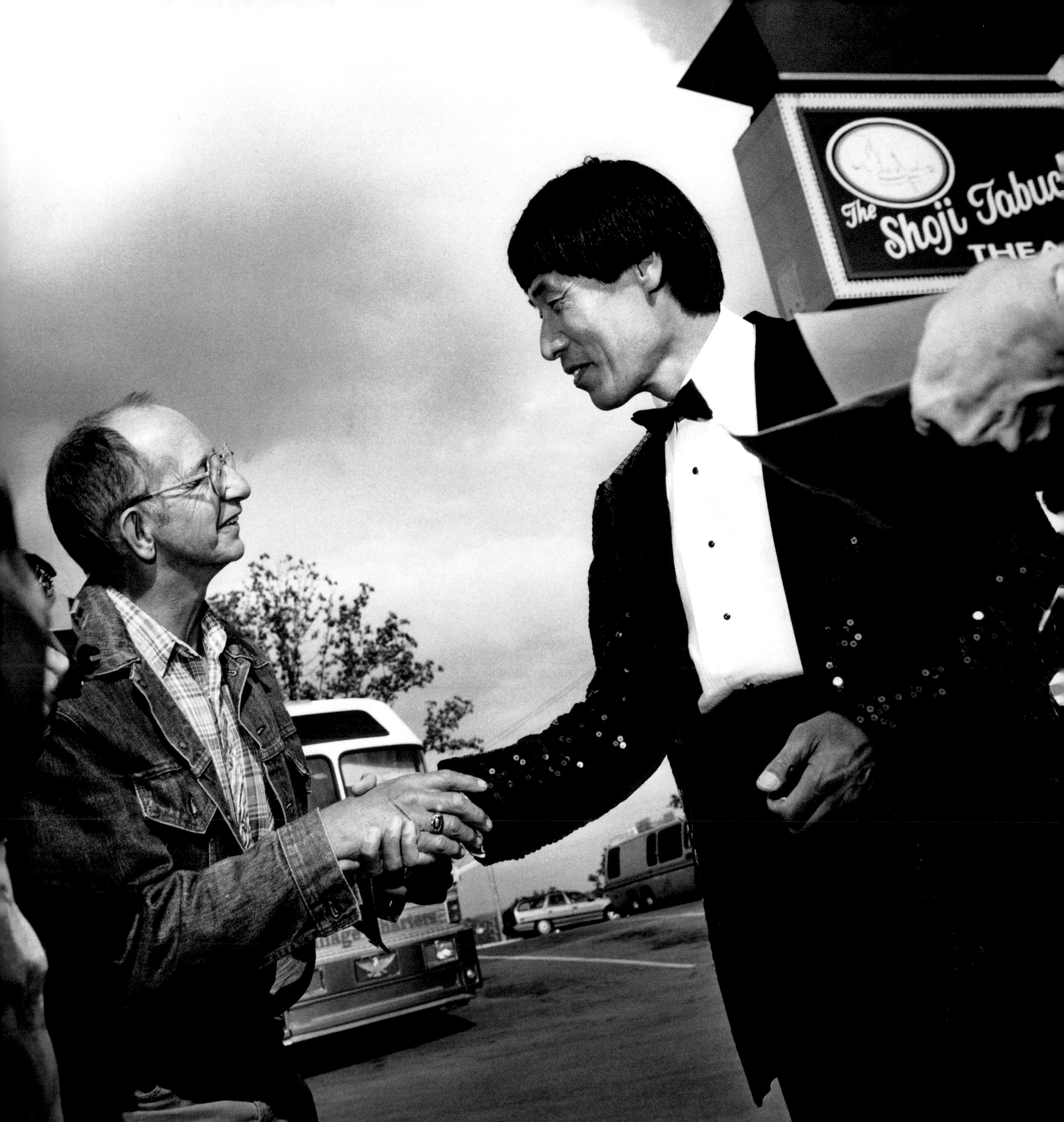
The Shoji

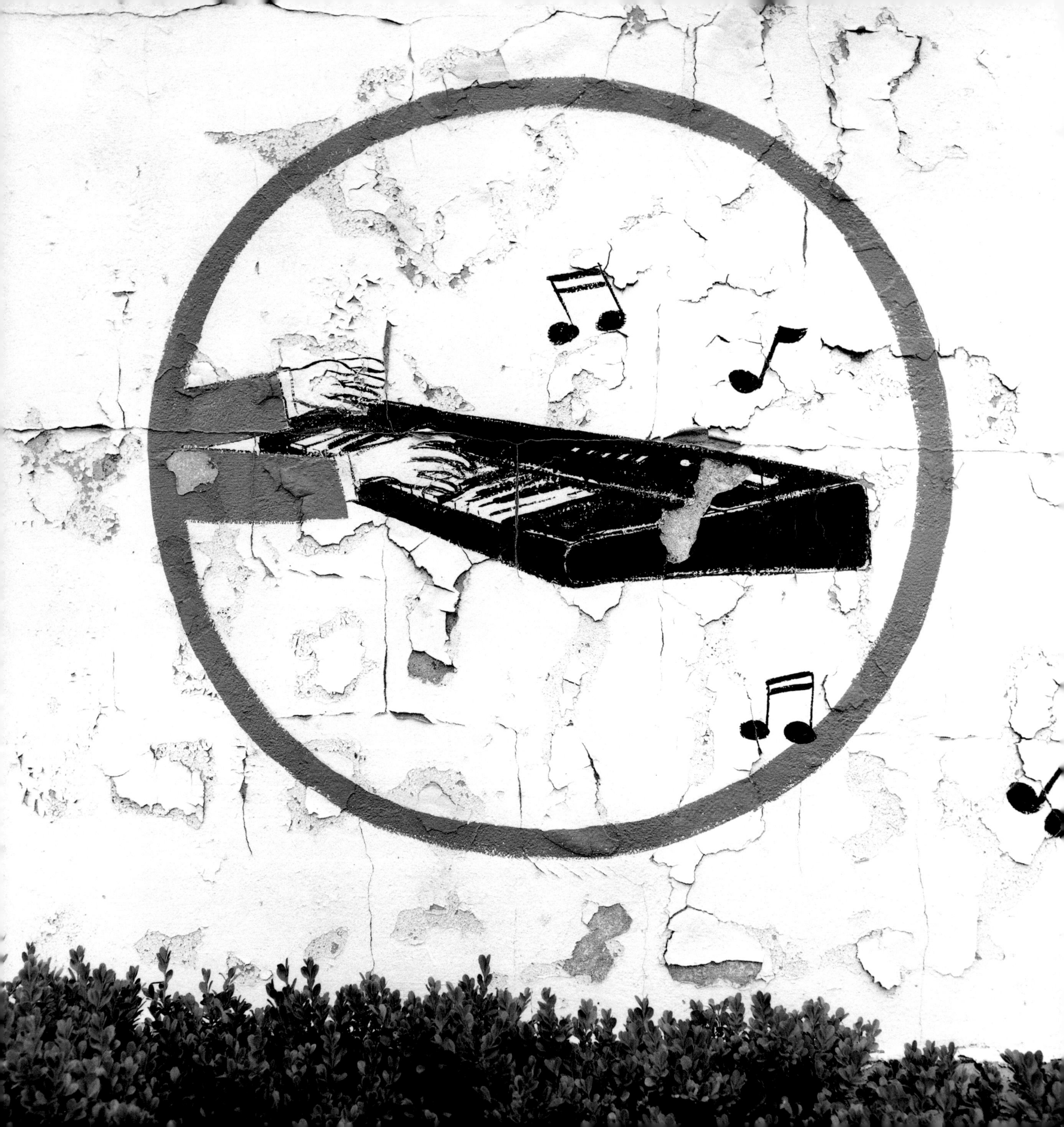

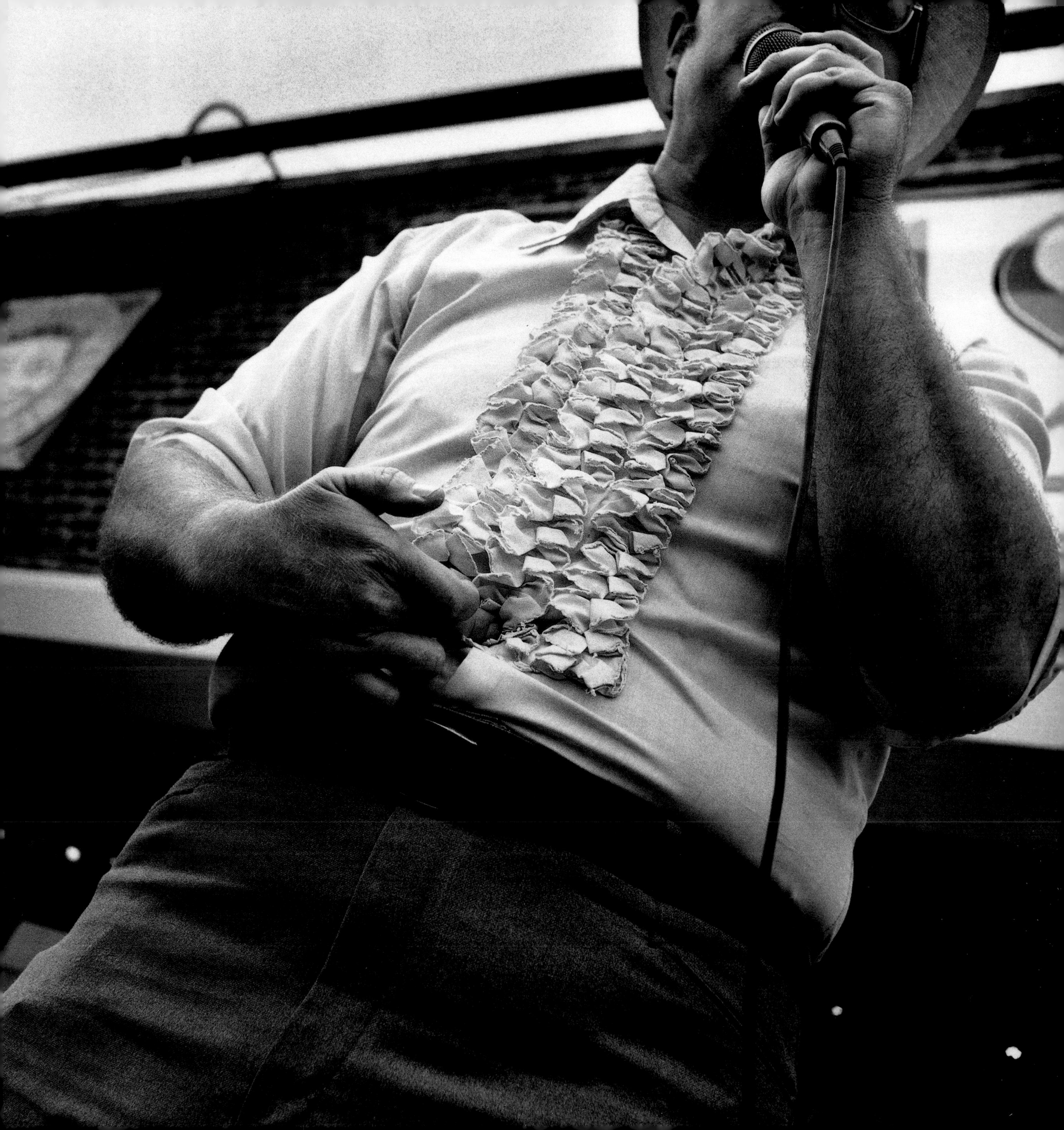

Willie Nelson after his concert,
Branson, Missouri, **1993**

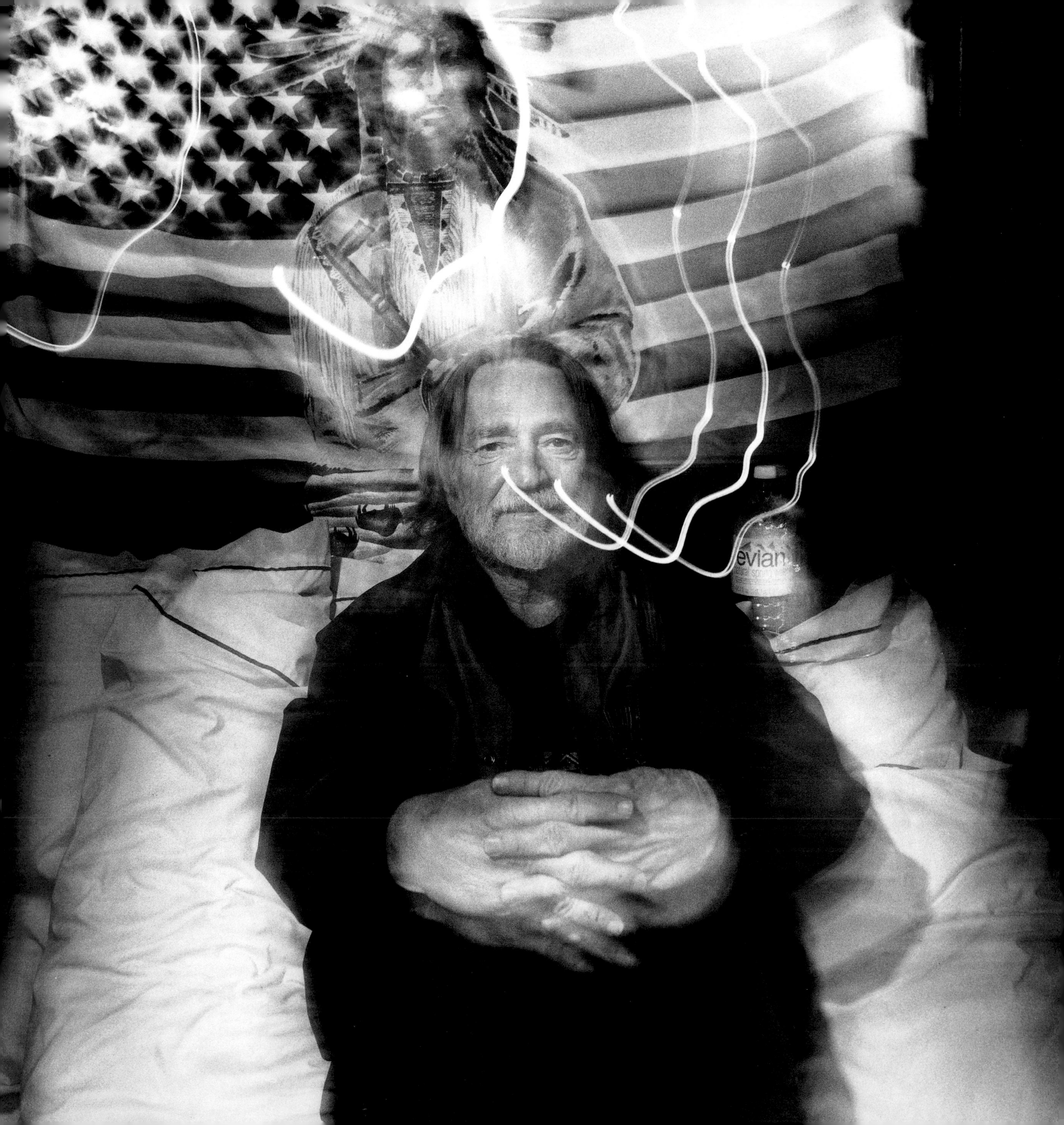
evian

Angel in Central Park, New York City, **1996**

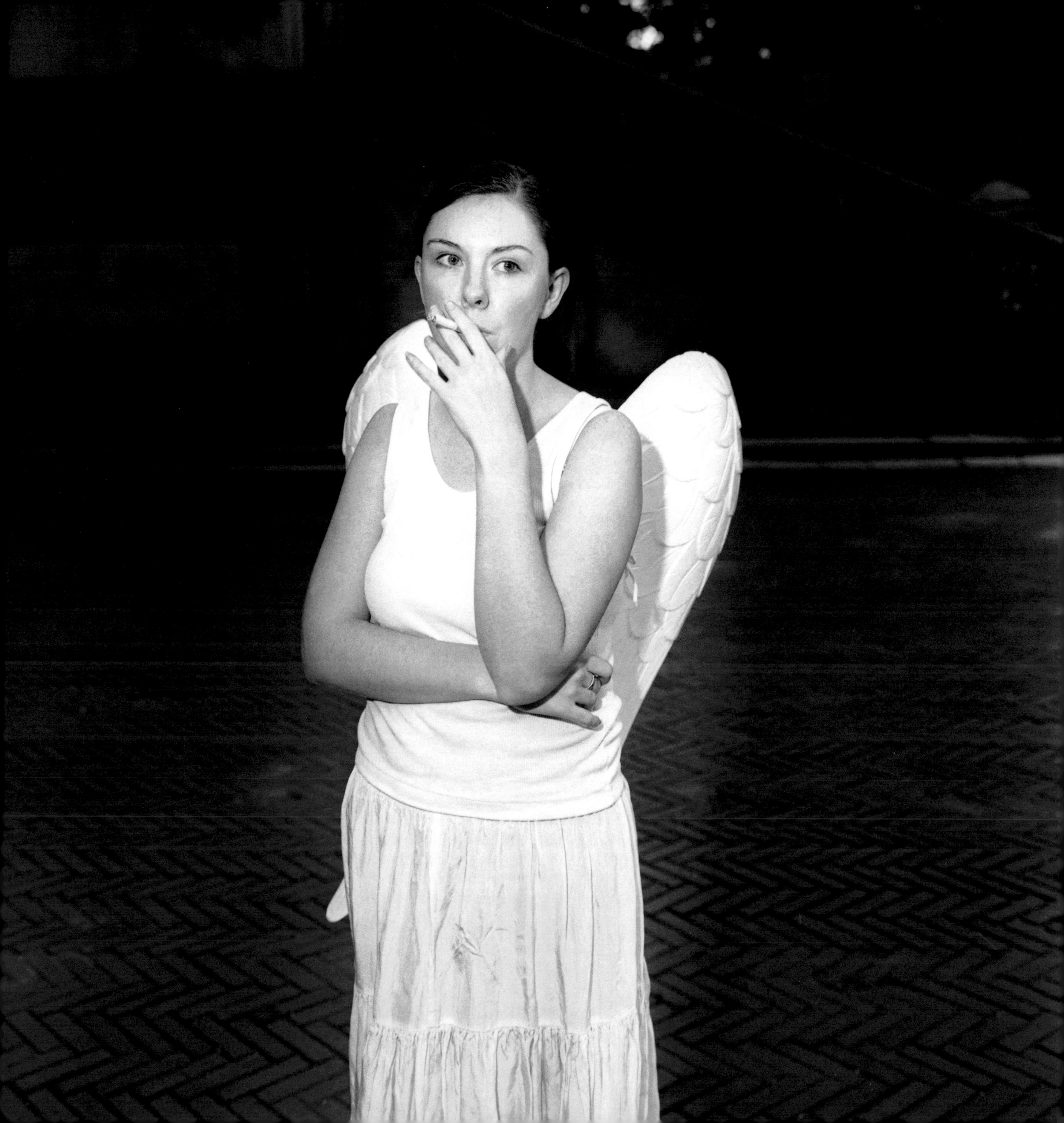

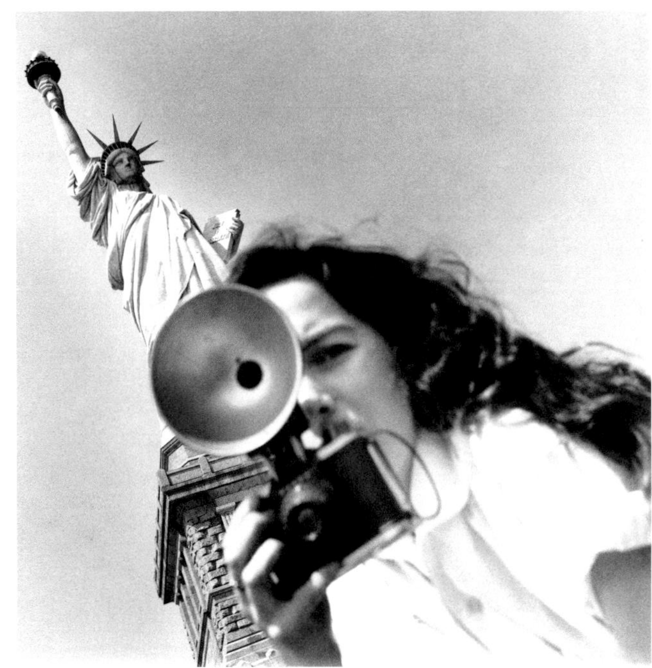

Self-portrait, New York City, **1990**

JOURNAL 1989-1997

Bastienne Schmidt

Shortly before my first visit to New York – that was in 1989 – I tried to put together an image of America for myself in my dreams. In one dream I strolled across a snow-white square, empty of people, in the glaring sunlight. The Manhattan skyline rose shining in the background, encased in a deep blue sky. I had simply put the expectations and fears I had of this new continent and this colossal city out of my mind. What appeared in my dream was a photograph that I was later to rediscover over and over again in the course of my various travels.

I found the drive to the East Village was an eerie experience. It was late at night; we drove past glowing fires at which people appeared to be cooking along the highway. They were surrounded by shopping carts packed full of all sorts of things – and plastic bags, shoes, personal belongings. It struck me as a kind of underworld. My cousin was waiting for me in her East Village studio on 6th Street. As I remember, we went out to an Indian restaurant to eat.

I spent the next few months getting up early. It was a beautiful fall, and the crystal clear light made everything I experienced in New York seem part of a fantasy world. I left the house every morning at eight to take photographs in the streets: the many different faces of people on their way to work, the rush and hurry of the New Yorkers, their obsessive drive, their positive attitude towards life – it was all quite fascinating at first, because I wasn't a part of it.

I made an effort to find my way in the world of photography, between jobs as a lab technician and an assistant. But my real love was the city of New York; Broadway, the different neighborhoods of Brooklyn, the many parallel worlds I explored on my photographic excursions.

I took some time before I discovered my interest in the rest of America. That began with trips that took me into the "Dutch" Amish country and to Atlantic City. At first I was appalled at the endless stretches of chain stores, shopping malls, neon signs, McDonalds restaurants, motels and filling stations along the highways. Where were the centers of towns? What was there for me to fix my gaze upon? There was so much information to take in and digest within a matter of seconds that everything flowed together into a film – a film that reminded me of the images of America I had seen on television: a fast-moving, consumption-oriented America. In the beginning I found it hard to take photographs, as I was accustomed to the distrustful looks of people in Germany. Here, however, curiosity with respect to new encounters seemed to get the better of any mistrust there might have been.

Over the years – on a number of long trips, some of which I undertook in connection with assignments for the *Frankfurter Allgemeine Magazin* – I had become a collector of photographic moments. My gaze followed my curiosity and the desire to understand American society and its rituals – both the everyday and the unusual ones.

ALL THE WORLD IS A STAGE

Branson, Missouri, 1992

Life in America turns out to be rather complicated for people who don't drive. I take a bus via Springfield to Branson, Missouri. Rooms are booked solid there throughout the year, mostly by family tourists and groups traveling by bus, people who spend a week in Branson listening to a constant diet of the melodious sounds of the newest country-and-western songs. I have a room in a motel at the edge of town, directly opposite the theater owned by Sohji Tabuchi, the "fantastic fiddler" from Japan.

A number of country-and-western stars, including Johnny Cash, Willie Nelson, Mel Tillis and Sohji Tabuchi have built their own theaters in Branson, where they play for three or four months every year when they are not on tour. When the stars are on tour, there is little opportunity for contact with their audiences. Branson's appeal is closeness to the stars. They are there in the flesh, available for photographs and autographs. Willie Nelson becomes a living photo opportunity and a friend of the family in one, because he poses so nicely with Mom, Dad and the kids. Nobody seems to mind at all that he sells three CDs and a ceramic mug with his picture on it in the process.

On my first day I wander along Highway 76, where all of the action is focused. My chamber of commerce pamphlet tells me that there are 35 theaters on Highway 76 alone – in addition to the twenty putt-putt golf courses, fountains, go-cart tracks, souvenir shops, fast-food chain outlets and motels. Cars are backed up bumper-to-bumper on both lanes of the road. Sweaty, round-cheeked faces stare at me through the car windows, wondering what in the world a pedestrian is doing there. The long line of cars moves at a snail's pace towards the theaters. A man and a woman, surely over seventy years old, laugh as they pass the standing cars on their motorcycle.

The audience slowly drifts into the Sohji Tabuchi Theater. I follow the stream of female spectators into the restroom. We are received there by a young woman dressed in black and wearing a white apron with frills. She is pushing a small cart full of pleasant scents, cremes, cotton balls and violets. "Ohs" and "ahs" are heard from in front of the gold-plated mirrors and the copper-plated water faucets: "It looks so pretty. I wish I could have that at home ..." Plastic chandeliers hang from the ceiling; an angel smiles down from the wallpaper.

Sohji appears on stage. He welcomes individual groups of bus travelers, his friends from Virginia and Tennessee, to the well-wishing applause of his audience. Sohji plays his virtuoso fiddle pieces wearing a silver-sequined jacket. His musical talent has the electrifying effect of circus acrobatics. The audience is totally enthused. After each song we learn a little more about Sohji's career: how he arrived in Nashville, poor, with only a suitcase in his hand, unable to speak a word of English but with the love of country music in his blood. And how it went from there: step by step, the first Japanese performer in the history of country-and-western music, the fastest, the greatest, the best ... a genuine American success story – from rags to riches. The audience nods in appreciation. There is great admiration for people who actually live the American dream. After the performance Sohji Tabuchi walks out to the bus to say goodbye to his friends, the bus travelers from Tennessee. Most of the people standing around are married couples, middle-aged and up. A man in a denim jacket wearing a signet ring shakes Sohji's hand firmly. Admiration and blind devotion are written all over his face. After everyone has had a chance to take Mr. Tabuchi's picture, the group happily gets onto the bus. Sohji plays a farewell melody for them.

There is also a wax museum on Highway 76 that claims to tell the history of the world in wax. I discover Marlene Dietrich, whom I wouldn't have recognized without her name plaque. She is in the company of President Roosevelt, Hitler, Elvis Presley, Dracula, Jesus and the Apostles at the Last Supper and Jackie Kennedy with her children. It's a small world in Branson. Good and evil stand side by side. The main thing is to be famous.

After four days of Highway 76, twelve meals in the "All you can eat for 10 dollars" restaurants, seven concerts featuring some good and some not so good country-and-western music and after visiting amusement parks and wild-west towns, I long for peace and quiet. As a gesture of farewell I have my picture taken at the Gizmek Wild West Photo Studio, dressed as a cowboy with a sack full of gold on the table. And that's all that counts, ultimately: cash and fun.

IN THE FIELD OF FIRE *Camp Perry, Cleveland, Ohio, 1992*

We're flying rather low, don't you think?" says the lady sitting next to me on the flight to Cleveland. "You can see everything perfectly." I nod my head. After uttering a few polite platitudes she lets the cat out of the bag: "May I ask you something? Are you familiar with the Bible?" From her handbag she pulls two little pamphlets with naively drawn renditions of scenes from a paradise on earth. "Have you ever heard of Jehovah's Witnesses," she asks. An airplane is a perfect place to attempt a conversion. There is no way to escape. "We are going to experience paradise on earth, the Kingdom of God," my neighbor tells me. The place I am on my way to visit is a shooting camp about an hour away from Cleveland, an event organized by the National Rifle Association. I ask the woman next to me if that is how she imagines paradise on earth, which seems to silence her.

Mr. Roberts, who is in charge of public relations for the National Rifle Association, greets me at Camp Perry. Camp Perry was established in 1906 after the Spanish-American War under law passed by Congress calling for enhanced military training opportunities for the civilian population. It served as a prisoner of war camp during the Second World War.

Today the annual national pistol and rifle shooting championship is being held here. Entire families gather for the occasion and travel here from every state of the Union. For a full week they live under conditions reminiscent of a boy scout camp, in tents and modest huts, come rain or come shine. And it is indeed a paradise on earth for them.

I am awakened on the first morning by strange sounds. It sounds as if someone were trying to start a car: a small burst, like an explosion, repeated over and over again. Mr. Roberts explains that this is the sound made by high-powered rifles. The competitors' task is to fire off as many shots as possible in sixty seconds, he says.

On the second day breakfast is served at 5:30 a.m. I am surrounded by a forest of flags in the breakfast room – each participant has brought along an American flag. Although it is raining cats and dogs, everyone is in good spirits. Packed into combat boots, water-tight overalls and camouflage raincoats, the families stomp through the mud with their high-powered rifles and their camping stools, accompanied by carts full of cleaning utensils and ammunition. The rain refuses to let up, and the decision is made to postpone the competition for three hours. Yet everyone stays put on their stools. Hoods pulled up over their heads, people sit around exchanging shooting stories.

I chat with a couple of 14-year-olds from Utah. They are wearing shorts and sweatshirts, one bearing the imprint "USA," and look very young. One of the girls recites the first rule of rifle safety she learned from her grandfather: "Never point your weapon at another person." The grandfather had then used a watermelon to demonstrate to her what happens to a human being hit by a rifle bullet. The watermelon had exploded on the bullet's violent impact. The girls seem quite mature for their age. "Once you've started shooting with a high-powered rifle it's like you're addicted to it. Normal pistol shooting is boring by comparison," says one girl earnestly. The other one continues: "Pistol marksmen are weaklings. They can't stand the rain, and they even complain about the sun. But high-powered rifle marksmen know that they can't complain." Their rifles look big and heavy, too heavy to be held in the arms of 14-year-old girls.

Like golf caddies, the participants pull their carts behind them to the next line of targets. The rifles are cleaned and put together at the assembly line. At the shooting line, the marksmen wait for the starting signal. All of a sudden shots begin to explode from all sides. This is what war sounds like, I imagine. I sense a rising primal fear that someone might accidentally point a weapon in the wrong direction, and I would be totally helpless.

People ask me again and again what I am doing here. "Hello, nice to meet you." Friendly faces talk about army assignments in Wiesbaden and Neu Ulm. They mention visiting the Heidelberg Castle and tell how much they enjoyed everything in Germany, especially the beer, the sausages and the Oktoberfest. A ten-year-old asks me whether the people from the former GDR come from a lower social class.

Mr. Roberts introduces me to a devoted lady marksman, a woman over eighty years of age: Alice Bull started shooting when she was just seven years old. I take her photograph, standing and sitting, but always with her rifle. This fragile-looking woman has come this time to accept an honorary award.

The Director of Civilian Marksmanship distributes the prizes and awards that evening. But first everyone rises, baseball caps pressed to their hearts, to sing the National Anthem. Then they pray together: Thank you for letting us take aim and shoot. And if we miss, we shall try to be modest. Oh my God, Amen!

A FENCE AT THE BORDER *San Diego, California, 1992*

At the San Isidro Border Station, just a few minutes away from the Mexican border, we visit Mr. Harding, an agent with the American border patrol. We drive along the border in his pick-up truck. A rusty metal fence, no more than three meters high, winds its way through the sandy landscape. This is how the U.S. protects itself against illegal immigrants. There are huge holes in the fence here and there. From behind one of these openings peers the head of a Mexican merchant, a man selling *tortas*, drinks, fresh fruits and second-hand clothing under a parasol. He sits on the Mexican side in Tijuana and has a view of the San Isidro plateau in the U.S. The place is also called Vista del Rio – view of the river. The man's business is not bad. There are about thirty people gathered around him. They are waiting for darkness to fall. Old carpets have been spread out for the night sleepers. I speak to a few people in Spanish. Their mistrust is impossible to overlook, as we are traveling with the *Migra*, their name for the border patrol. "Your border patrolman is one of the nicer ones," a man tells me. "There are lots of them that beat people up before deporting them." The border patrolman, in turn, complains that they don't have enough money or people to seal off the border to the illegal *pollos* – chickens, as they refer to the border-crossers.

We spend the next day in Tijuana, on the Mexican side of the border. Entering from the U.S. side is child's play. A crowd of people returning from San Isidro to Mexico squeezes through the metal gateway, similar to a subway exit. There is no passport control. The travelers are loaded with plastic bags and bulky cardboard boxes full of household appliances and electronic gear. I look into the faces. It is absolutely impossible to distinguish the legals from the illegals.

From a bridge in the center of Tijuana one can look down at the old canal of the Rio Grande, the geographic boundary that separates Mexico and the U.S. The American border fence stands directly behind the canal. The riverbed is dry. Countless people are standing or sitting near the fence, waiting in its shadow for darkness to come. Among them are quite a few men between the ages of 15 and 25 from every region of Mexico – Michoacan, Oaxaca, Guadalajara. Some of them have made their own way to Tijuana; others have entered into deals with the *coyotes*, the immigrant smugglers, who arrange for the entire trip. Some have gone deep into debt before even setting foot on American soil. No one wants to be photographed. Vittorio, a street photographer, tells horror stories of attacks on people trying to cross the border. "This is a no-man's land. Who is going to protect these people here against criminals?" He tells of a seventeen-year-old girl who was raped as her parents looked on. Another customary practice, he says, is robbery committed on refugees, who usually carry the few dollars they possess on their person.

The Mexican government has established a new border police organization, the "Beta Group," which is responsible for protecting the lives of refugees. A border patrolman in the Beta Group earns about a thousand dollars, a substantial salary in Mexico. As a result, police corruption is not an issue. The Mexican officers also cooperate with the American side.

There are five major crossing points for illegal immigrants: at Borderfield State Park, at Bronxville, at "The Dairy Matt," in "Smuggle Canyon" and in the "Canyon of the Killers." There are also a number of theories about which point is the easiest to cross. Jack, an American border patrolman, estimates that between 300 and 400 people cross the border every night. It is not difficult to get past the border fence. People climb it and jump to the other side or dig holes beneath it. In fact, the fence itself is not the real barrier. The cat-and-mouse game begins behind it. Refugees move quietly across the terrain like thieves in the night in groups of 15 to 20. The American border police can detect every movement with their infrared cameras. Equipped with two-way radios, the patrolmen communicate with one another, dispatching their watch partners in pursuit of the border-crossers. "The frustrating thing about it," says Jack, "is that for every one we intercept at least three others make it to the U.S. And if they don't get there tonight, they'll try again tomorrow." What sounds like a game during the day becomes hard reality at night. Cars full of illegals are unloaded at the border station. The people's faces show their exhaustion. Many of them are women and children. They are deported the same night.

We spend Sunday in Borderfield State Park. Families gather here for picnics, mango-sellers have set up stands, and there is a Mexican band playing. The idyllic appearance is an illusion. It is said that forged identity cards are sold in the public toilets, that marijuana is sold here. "You can believe about half of what people tell you," the mango-seller claims with a wink. The park lies on the Mexican border. A great many people on both sides converse across the fence. I learn later that the somewhat heavy-set lady in the stretch pants is a coyote, an immigrant smuggler. She is said to have earned enough money through her profession to buy several houses. From time to time someone tries to slip through a hole to the American side, but a border patrolman is on scene immediately.

The fence ends down at the beach. Sandra sits with her family having a picnic. She lives in the U.S., where she earns more than her husband, who is still in Mexico. Today she has sat down with her children on the American side, while her husband has his meal on the Mexican side. They meet here every Sunday. It is normally forbidden to exchange food across the border, but Sandra places the tacos precisely in the middle – in the no-man's land. The border patrolmen seem not to mind. Late in the afternoon the park is closed. Entire families are already waiting on the beach to try their luck tonight.

MEXICANS IN LOS ANGELES *Los Angeles, California, 1992*

From the airplane I can see rows of houses and swimming pools, embedded in a tangle of countless intersecting highways. The cars below move forward at a snail's pace. They remind me of plasma flowing through the veins of the city. This is the pulse of Los Angeles.

J. B. picks me up at the airport, and we make our way to the hotel. I find Los Angeles oppressive. The trip downtown takes us through Mission Street. We drive past dilapidated buildings and people crouching around fires. I see sleeping quarters built of cardboard and a few tents. The first large camp for illegal immigrants near the border is located in Los Angeles. There is not much that looks American in downtown Los Angeles. Broadway could just as well be in Mexico City. A bus takes people from here straight to the Mexican border for ten dollars. A flight to Mexico City costs a hundred dollars. The air around me is filled with fragments of Spanish sentences and salsa music. Even the street signs and signs in the shops are in Spanish. An attorney promises, in Spanish, confidentiality and a solution for every green-card problem. The Estrellas Bakery next door advertises "No. 1 en pan mexicano," the only real Mexican bread. Just about everything here is reasonably priced. The cheapest articles in the second-hand shops cost around a dollar. A complete outfit with gold sequins can be had for as little as five dollars.

Above the stores are the sweatshops where the new immigrants work. Many of the owners are immigrants themselves, who put the newcomers to work for less than four dollars an hour. Women sit at long tables sewing zippers into brand-name jeans. The Korean proprietor quickly sends me out the door.

I eat a taco and ask a Mexican what he thinks is typical for a Mexican in Los Angeles. He responds: "What is typical is not the unusual but the norm. More than half of the population speaks Spanish. We are the silent majority." I speak Spanish with him. The language we share opens a door of trust. He talks of discrimination and segregation at the hands of both whites and African Americans. They refer to themselves as "Chicanos," as the expression "Hispanic" has been given negative connotations by the "Anglos." The Chicanos live in Boyle Heights. East Los Angeles is home to both African Americans and Chicanos. Huntington Park is Chicano territory. Beverly Hills is white. Each of these areas is separated from the others by freeways. The life that goes on in a neighboring section passes by like the images in a movie. These are parallel worlds in which no one knows the others.

I visit Olvera Street, described in the tourist guide as the oldest authentic Hispanic street. It turns out to be a tourist trap, a place where Mexican flags and tee-shirts with death-heads are sold. There I meet Isabel, who has just arrived from El Paso with her three-year-old son a few days before. She has all of their belongings with her in two carrier bags. Isabel is looking for work. "Any job," she says, "because I want to pay off the debts on my house in Cancun. I've come only to earn money." She took care of three children in El Paso, earning 120 dollars a week. It was a job that allowed her to take her son Diego along. Her biggest problem here will be to find another job where she can take her son to work with her. She doesn't really care much for North America. The stories are all alike: the move to *el Norte* is undertaken for economic reasons.

Isabel stands in line with other people in front of the La Plazita Church, the oldest and largest Mexican church in Los Angeles. Paul Molina, a church social worker, distributes coupons. At least thirty people come here every day. Paul offers them a lunch and a coupon for a week's accommodation in a refuge for the homeless. He explains how difficult things are for the immigrants at first, as the newcomers attempt to survive on the streets of Los Angeles without speaking a word of English. I read in the *Los Angeles Times* about a twenty-year-old boy from Purissima in Mexico, who crossed the border illegally with twenty dollars in his shoe. He worked without a permit, saved his money and had enough to enable his parents to put an addition on their house. Then he was seriously injured in a traffic accident. His mother journeyed from Mexico to take her now paraplegic, mentally disabled son back home. "El Norte is taking away our children and our dreams. We built a new room in our house, but for what?" Nevertheless, the mother accepts her fate with the help of her faith in God.

Mary Ann Diaz is a former member of a Chicano gang. Now she is working on a project devoted to helping girls free themselves from gang ties. The brutality of the Mexican gangs is a rapidly spreading phenomenon. Twenty-eight people were shot to death last weekend alone. One of them was an ice-cream seller, mugged in the center of town (for the twenty dollars he had in his pocket). Parents' dreams of giving their children a better life have turned into nightmares.

Mary Ann regards herself as a Chicano – her parents are from Mexico – but speaks no Spanish. She doesn't care for Mexican men, because she finds their macho ways too much to bear. Her boyfriend is an American. She feels genuinely at home nowhere. Called a "gringa" during her vacation in Mexico, she is looked on as a Hispanic in the U.S. She first attempted to develop a sense of cultural identity through the gang. She says: "Columbus Day? We're supposed to celebrate that? That's a farce to us. Who remembers the losers on that day – the Native Indians and the Mexicans who thought of this country as their home just a hundred years ago?"

Group baptisms are celebrated in the La Plazita Church on every second Saturday. The whole family gathers in the church courtyard. The women are dressed for the occasion, with their prim hairdos, their make-up and their mini-skirts. The children's ages range from ten months to five years. The boys wear lily-white mini-tuxedos, the girls shiny satin dresses. Most of them have a small, ornamental crucifix around their necks, a gift of their god-parents. The fathers stand around with their oversized video cameras and record this first big milestone in life. After the baptism ceremony, everyone poses for a paid photographer. Their faces are full of happiness and pride.

OBSESSED WITH SKIN AND HAIR

Beverly Hills, California, 1993

Three maids are busy preparing the Presidential Suite on the top floor of the Beverly Wiltshire Hotel: a hallway, one room giving way to the next – each furnished with large porcelain lamps, darkly stained cocktail tables, sofas, chandeliers and starched curtains. The maids are dark-skinned and dressed in white aprons. They come from El Salvador and Mexico. They dust, change the soap and puff up the pillows. A night here costs over 1000 dollars. Young-looking, well-dressed people sit in the hotel café. The soft but insistent beeping of cell telephones is a standard feature in the mix of background sound. Most of the women boast stiff, blonde manes of hair. They show their immaculate teeth when they smile, bleached white, of course. Every move is intended to draw attention. Producers, Hollywood agents and film-makers gather at this hotel to do business over lunch or dinner.

Rodeo Drive, the most expensive shopping boulevard in the world, begins across from the hotel. Hordes of tourists storm into Giorgio's to buy perfumes and colognes. Germans pass by, carrying their travel guides and MCM bags. Yet Rodeo Drive has become a tourist myth, since the stars prefer to shop in the anonymity of the malls. One designer boutique after the other – Beverly Hills taste is loud and brightly colored. A few galleries are interspersed among the boutiques, full of art as colorful as it is tasteless.

Parallel to Rodeo Drive runs a commercial street with the addresses of plastic surgeons, hairstylists, drugstores and attorneys. José Eber's Hair Salon is located in a small street that angles off from Rodeo Drive. José, the master hairstylist, makes his appearance. He hides his long, meticulously groomed hair beneath a cowboy hat, which reappears as a leitmotif in the form of a sombrero with red velvet upholstery – a divan right in the middle of the salon. Ten young-looking hairstylists broadcast good cheer and pleasant vibrations. They are at work cutting the hair of a row of middle-aged women. José is the recognized darling of the TV talk shows. He is frequently invited to appear with Jenny or Leeza to give women a free makeover on the show. I remember one episode of Leeza's talk show. A series of average women of varying ages is introduced, all in denim jackets and jeans and without make-up – women just released from prison. Within half an hour José manages to turn them into modern, good-looking young women. The audience shows its appreciation. José waves kisses at them. It is said that Burt Reynolds has his hair cut at José Eber's salon. But don't the gossip columnists claim that Burt wears a toupee?

Americans are obsessed with their hair. I see practically nothing but men with thick hair and not a trace of gray, which prompts me to take a look at their hairlines, a sure way to pick out a toupee-wearer. Even the television news anchormen seem to have grown more hair rather than less as each year passes. Hair on the head is considered a status symbol and a sign of success. Body hair, on the other hand, is frowned upon.

We make a visit to a real estate agent for the rich and the stars. She wants to give us a look at the living habits of the rich in Beverly Hills. She talks in a constant stream. Her enthusiasm appears somewhat routine, practiced. She juggles two receivers while she speaks on the telephone with potential clients. Her life fits the pattern of a Danielle Steele novel: She was married to a Hollywood star, wrote a best-seller during the seventies and now sells houses and lots. She wears a tight-fitting, beige leather suit studded with gold buttons. Her hair is peroxide blonde and her face covered with a thick layer of make-up. The pressure to achieve success is immense. What counts is the façade: chest out, head up! Life is a great big show. On the next day, we drive with her and an architect friend into Beverly Hills. We stop in front of Rod Stewart's still unfinished house. A classical characteristic of the American ideal of luxury is the number of bathrooms and walk-in closets a home has. Every bedroom must have its own bathroom and an immense closet. A swimming pool is a must. But large fireplaces and kitchens done in granite are also in demand. The house

Sylvester Stallone almost bought has similar features. The agent poses for me on the elegantly winding marble stairway in the foyer.

After Beverly Hills I take time to enjoy Venice Beach, just a few miles away. Families drive to the beach on the weekend. It does one good to see the rounded bodies playing in the water. Beauty and ugliness unite in a thoroughly natural way here. Real life takes place here, on the beach.

THE DEATH BED

Huntsville, Texas, 1995

Sam Houston, founding father of the state of Texas, stands as a gigantic sculpture greeting motorists along Highway 45 on the route to Huntsville. The Huntsville Prison is located in the middle of the city, three blocks from the church and four from the candy store. Hunstville looks like a sleepy little town. But its life is closely connected with the prison that forms the basis of the local economy.

The majority of the people here have no interest in discussing the death penalty. As one college girl explains: "It's the norm that people here are for the death penalty. I really haven't ever thought much about it. When someone commits a crime, he should consider the consequences. Why should we waste our tax money to keep criminals in prison for life? It's an eye for an eye." This archaic definition of right and wrong seems to be widely accepted here.

We visit Larry Fitzgerald, who coordinates public relations for the prison in Huntsville. Larry is an amiable man about forty years of age, a guy one would never imagine occupying such a position. He informs us that an execution is to take place at six o'clock that evening. From his computer he prints out a list of people already executed. The administration of death by government order is painstaking and precise: The death row inmate's number and the chronological serial number of his execution is listed next to his name and age on the date of execution. The 101st execution is to take place this evening. The record will also contain details of the convict's last meal and his last spoken words. It is a bureaucratic ritual with almost biblical character.

On the following day we visit the Ellis Unit, an auxiliary facility outside the prison, where the death row prisoners are housed. A prison guard lowers a plastic bucket from a watchtower. We drop our passports and identity cards into it. Through several rows of waist-high fences supplemented by coils of barbed wire I see a crèche scene. The baby Jesus is lying on the grass, with Mary and Joseph at his side ... It is not long till Christmas. The entrance is decorated with Christmas stars and tinsel and reminds one more of a school than a prison. A framed photograph of Mr. Ellis, the prison founder, hangs as a focal point on the entrance wall. The faces of his successors surround his picture. The flags of the United States and the state of Texas have been set up to the right and left of the portraits.

We have been given permission to interview two death row inmates. The visitors' side of the waiting room is furnished with a long row of chairs. A Coca-Cola machine stands at one end of the room. Visitors are separated from the inmates by a bullet-proof pane of glass reinforced with wire mesh. T. sits opposite us in small cell, his head practically pressing against the glass. We are hesitant and uneasy at first. "Nice to meet you ..." We couldn't shake his hand even if we wanted to. His execution date has been set for January 31st. He has less than a month left to live. He is convicted of having been involved, together with his wife, in a jewelry store robbery during which a person was killed. He denies all guilt, claiming that the police identified the wrong man.

The death penalty allows no leeway for judicial error. Yet most of those condemned to death belong to ethnic minorities, primarily low-income segments of the population. They are often people with extremely low IQs, which causes one to wonder about the fairness of justice. T., an African American, is not a wealthy man. He has a captivating manner in conversation. There is wisdom in his eyes. "You don't have any real friends in prison. The battlefronts are constantly changing, depending on what favors you do for whom. My only friends are my wife and a girl who helps me deal with the judicial bureaucracy. The psychological torture is not knowing when it's going to happen. The execution date has already been postponed several times in response to an appeal. The last time I had already been moved to the death cell when the stay came through, and they took me back just seven hours before the scheduled time of execution. But how long can that go on?" T. does not want to die. He rages against the American justice system, calling it unfair, discriminatory and impossible to beat. "Without money you can't afford a good lawyer. And without a lawyer you don't have a chance."

A guard takes us to the cells on death row. We enter a long hallway with three cubicles on each side. The cells are furnished with beds and toilets. The TV sets mounted in the hallway are on, but the sound has been turned off. Ricki Lane's talk show is running on the flickering TV screen. From the subtitles I can decipher the words "guns," "death" and "violence." All of the cells have been opened towards the front, so that the guards have a view inside. The guards tell us that they frequently find handmade weapons, pistols carved out of soap sometimes, or forks bent to shape. There are no limits to the inmates' imagination. Some of the prisoners have placed mirrors between the steel bars, enabling them to communicate with their neighbors in adjacent cells. They make unmistakable comments and laugh as I walk along the hallway.

Larry shows us the execution cell. The place reminds me of a hospital room somewhere in the suburbs, painted in a bluish tone and totally impersonal. In the middle of the room stands a white-sheeted bed with handmade leather straps and extended armrests. A microphone has been placed above the bed to record the condemned man's last words. Later in the evening, volunteers will do the necessary work in the next room. They will inject saline solutions through several different ampules into the condemned man's arm. One of them will contain the fatal dosage, but no one will know who actually administered it. It is a form of anonymous killing without personal accountability. In a room adjacent to the execution cell, separated from it by a wall of glass, the relatives of the condemned inmate have traditionally gathered to watch the execution. In the future the room is to be divided. Separated by a single wall, the relatives of the both the victims *and* the killers will be able to witness the execution.

Two executions are to take place at six o'clock that evening. We wait alongside a small group of demonstrators and opponents of the death penalty beneath the prison clock. I am overcome by a sad sense of helplessness. I simply cannot believe that these deaths, ordained by the state, are inevitable. Two streets away, a Christmas procession moves through the city. Little girls in angel costumes stand on the back of pick-up trucks, singing. No one appears to have taken notice of the execution.

The burials take place early the next morning at the Joe Bird Cemetery, a prison burial ground on the outskirts of the city. It is open to the public. Convicts who die in the prison are interred here. If the family of the deceased is unable to pay for his funeral, he is registered at the cemetery as a number. The crosses marking the graves of executed convicts bear a black "X."

It starts to rain. A group of Vietnamese has gathered to witness the funeral of the first Vietnamese executed in the U.S. The funeral party sings Protestant hymns under their umbrellas. One of them tapes the event – a memento for the deceased's parents in Vietnam. White-clad convicts who serve as coffin-bearers and grave diggers take off their hats during the sermon. Their hands are folded.

A GREYHOUND BUS TRIP

From Salt Lake City to San Francisco, 1995

Nicely dressed young people stand in front of the Mormon Cathedral in Salt Lake City. They offer guided tours through the church in a variety of languages. The smiling women wear long dresses with floral patterns. The young girl who is our guide comes from Brazil. Her English has a warm sound. We walk through a large, sky-blue room with a ceiling covered with stars towards a huge sculpted figure of Christ. Later, we are shown a melodramatic film on the history of the Mormons. The ebullient friendliness of the people here is a little overwhelming.

The Greyhound bus station is only three blocks from the cathedral. People wait on the steps and inside the terminal for their busses to depart. There is a line of people at the ticket counter. The local times in New York, Los Angeles, Chicago and Salt Lake City are displayed above the counter next to the Greyhound logo. A number of different people have settled in the waiting room. A young mother, perhaps from Mexico, plays with her three children. She holds a four-month-old infant in her arms. A younger man with short, blonde hair and stubble on his chin lies across a row of seats, his roll-up sleeping bag serving as a pillow. He is asleep. A young couple lying on the floor snuggles closer together. The departure of the bus to Chicago is announced. People hurry to the exit.

For many people in search of something the Greyhound waiting room is both a transit point and a home. They are known as drifters or wanderers. They sleep in the streets, sometimes in refuges for the homeless or in Greyhound stations. I have encountered them on a number of journeys. They walk along the highways, attracting little notice. Their faces are deeply tanned, their hair matted and messy. They are a part of these forlorn American landscapes that have room for aimless wanderers. Our journey takes us to Idaho Falls, Butte, Spokane, Boise, Winnemucca, Reno and San Francisco. We stop overnight at hotels and climb into the next bus the following morning.

On the way to Spokane I chat with Hank, who has been on the road for a decade and now wants to settle down in Spokane. He hopes to start a new life – with a house, a wife and children. Hank doesn't look like a drifter. He is wearing a clean checkered shirt and jeans. Only his heavy walking shoes reveal his wandering ways. He tells how he gradually became a dropout from society. It all began with an injury at work and the subsequent loss of his job. Forced to move out of his apartment, he soon found himself on the road. Most people on the road are alone. Sometimes groups will form out of need. The drifters make do, taking seasonal jobs and panhandling. Hank's parents own a small farm, but their financial situation is bad, too. It is for their sake that he wants to make a new start. He gets off the bus in Spokane. By coincidence, I see him the next day in front of the refuge for the homeless. It is hard to find a new foothold in society.

The landscapes we pass seem endless. For the first time I have a sense of the vastness of the American continent. We ride through the forests of the Rocky Mountains. Landscapes open up and retreat again. The mountains give way to grassy green plateaus where cattle graze. Our way takes us over long stretches of countryside in which not a solitary soul is to be seen.

Another category of Greyhound travelers is comprised of elderly women. They like traveling by bus – perhaps because they are afraid to fly. They are retired, and they travel to visit their children and grandchildren. After a few hours on the bus, the seats are particularly uncomfortable for them. A young woman with a baby in her arms comes from Salt Lake City. She is moving – with a child and four boxes of belongings. She gets off the bus somewhere between Idaho Falls and Pocatello. No one is there to pick her up. Another mother, this one with three children, hails from Utah. Her ten-year-old son tells me his brief but dramatic life story. His father was arrested. The family was forced to sneak out of its house. There wasn't even time enough to pack, and his toys were left behind. Now they are on their way to move in with an aunt in Sacramento. They are looking forward to California. Their mother has already told them so much about it. During the trip the children eat peanut-butter sandwiches on soft, soggy white bread, their favorite food. An acrid smell comes from the toilets.

We travel across the desert. Arid and whitish-gray, it surrounds us in every direction. We approach Las Vegas. After the empty, silent landscape of the desert, the hustle and bustle here has the appearance of a mirage. The bus is cleaned in Las Vegas. The children play video games. I search desperately for something to eat, but aside from Coke and a few chips there is nothing to be had. I find the diffidence exhibited by most Americans with respect to food annoying. I long for a tasty, nutritious meal.

After a week of bus travel we arrive in San Francisco. The proximity to water has a calming effect. I take a deep breath of sea air.

CHRONOLOGY

1961: born April 3 in Munich, Germany
1969-79: lives and attends school in Athens, Greece
1980: returns to Munich to study ethnology at the Ludwig Maximilian University; works in a psychiatric hospital
1983: moves to Perugia, Italy, to study painting and photography at the Accademia di Belle Arti, Pietro Vannucci
1987: receives Bachelor of Fine Arts Degree; moves to New York City and begins work at the International Center of Photography; works for the photographer Ralph Gibson
1989-95: travels to Guatemala, Mexico, Colombia, Bolivia, Peru, Brazil and Cuba; starts work on the project *Vivir la Muerte*; regular contributor for magazines including the *Frankfurter Allgemeine Magazin*, *New York Times Magazine*, *The New Yorker* and *New York Magazine*
1992-97: travels to North America; starts work on the project *American Dreams*

Solo Exhibitions

1996 *Vivir la Muerte*, Blue Sky Gallery, Portland, Oregon; *Vivir la Muerte*, Chapel Art Center, Cologne, Germany; *Vivir la Muerte*, Haneburg-Leer, Germany; *Vivir la Muerte*, Houston Center for Photography, Houston, Texas; *Death Rituals*, Throckmorton, New York; *Vivre la mort*, Musée de la Photographie, Charleroi, Belgium
1995 *Fragments of Bogota*; *The New Documentarians*, International Center of Photography, New York
1993 *Vivir la Muerte*, Opsis-Foundation, New York
1992 *Storie di donne*, Galleria Planita, Rome, Italy; *Hunger, Art, Touch*, installations and photographs, Galería Libertadores, Lima, Peru; *Vivir la Muerte*, Galería Kahlo-Coronel, Mexico City
1991 *Memento mori*, photographs and objects, Alliance Française, Lima, Peru
1989 *Frammenti*, Galleria Atelier, Perugia, Italy

Group Exhibitions

1997 *The Garden of Eden*, Noorderlicht Festival, Groningen, The Netherlands
1996 *False Notions*, Nijmegen, The Netherlands; *20/20, Saint Barbara*, Contemporary Arts Forum, Santa Barbara, California; Center for Creative Photography, Tuscon, Arizona; *Discoveries of Fotofest*, Houston, Texas; *Latin American Photography*, Brooklyn Museum, New York; *Deutscher Fotojournalismus*, Deichtorhallen, Hamburg, Germany
1995 *On Death*, National Museum for Photography, Television and Broadcasting, Bradford, England; *Dia de los muertos*, Cable Access Gallery, Houston, Texas; *A Bestiarium*, Throckmorton, New York; *AFAP, Photography*, Prague, Czech Republic
1994 *The Photo-Essay*, Museum of Photography, Rotterdam, The Netherlands; *AFAP*, Julia Cameron House, Island of Wight, England; *German Photo Prize*, Stuttgart, Germany; *German Photo Prize*, Photokina, Cologne, Germany; *German Photojournalism*, Arles, France; *Dance of the Conquistadores*, Cavin Morris, New York
1993 *Compassion*, Hamilton Gallery, London; *World Press Photo*, Amsterdam, The Netherlands, Travelling exhibition
1991 *The Interrupted Life*, The New Museum, New York; *Portraits*, Brand Name Damage, New York
1990 *Current Directions*, Museum of Contemporary Hispanic Art, New York
1988 *Animalia*, Arpino, Italy; *Expo Bari*, Bari, Italy
1986 *Opere recenti dell'Accademia Pietro Vannucci*, Academy of Fine Arts, Krakow, Poland
1985 *Colori nel mondo*, Rocca Paolina, Perugia, Italy

Awards

1997 Irene Fromme Award, Snug Harbor Cultural Center, Staten Island, New York
1996 Kodak Fotobuch Preis for *Vivir la Muerte*, Stuttgart, Germany; Soros Foundation, Open Society Institute, Project on Death in America; In cooperation with the photographer Philippe Cheng
1993 Photoförderpreis, Landesgirokasse, Stuttgart, Germany
1992 2nd prize World Press Photo, Amsterdam, The Netherlands
1987 Award of the Academy of Fine Arts, Bari, Italy

Collections

Museum of Modern Art, New York; Brooklyn Museum, New York; International Center of Photography, New York; The Museum of Fine Arts, Houston, Texas; Center for Creative Photography, Tuscon, Arizona; Bibliothèque Nationale, Paris; Museet Fotografiska, Stockholm, Sweden; Corcoran Gallery of Arts, Washington, D.C.; Victoria and Albert Museum, London

ACKNOWLEDGMENT

I wish to thank first and foremost the people in the United States who permitted me to peer, for brief moments, into their lives. Thanks as well are due to my husband Philippe, with whom travelling is truly enjoyable, and to Antonio Todini, my photography teacher from Perugia.
I am grateful to Barbara Millstein from the Brooklyn Museum for her understanding and her interest in photography. Special thanks go to the *FAZ Magazin* and to Thomas Schröder, whose assignments helped make my journey through the breadth of America possible, and to Peter Breul, Monika Rettschnick and Robin Sanders.
I thank Kathy Ryan of the *New York Times Magazine* for her interest in the America project and Elizabeth Biondi of the *New Yorker* for her steadfast support. I am grateful as well to Mary Ellen Mark and Barry Taylor for many years of support and friendship.
To Jean Caslin of the Houston Center for Photography, Ed Osowski and Pampa Risso Patron go my thanks for help and guidance in Houston. I wish to thank the Project on Death in America of the Open Society Institute and Julie McCrady for their support as well. A word of thanks is also due to the Snug Harbor Cultural Center, to Olivia Georgia and Kay Takeda.
I would like to thank Ralph Gibson for his willingness to listen. Thanks to Charlie Steinback and the International Center of Photography, to Peter Nestler for his openness and his assistance in Cologne, Margie Goldberg of the *New York Magazine* and Sabine Meyer and Nak Yung Han for their support.
I am especially grateful to my New York gallery Throckmorton and to the Blue Sky Gallery in Portland. Thanks are due as well to Lookat, my agency in Switzerland.
Many thanks to Vicki Goldberg for her foreword and Hans-Georg Pospischil for his unflagging interest in photography and his belief in this project. I wish to thank Mirjam Ghisleni-Stemmle for her thoughtful, sensitive editing and Dr. Thomas N. Stemmle, who has not lost faith in pictures.
I thank my family: Sophie and Sebastian, Nicole and Benjamin, Aurelia and Florian, Pascale and Michael, the children Levin, Pauline, Marie, Julian and Freddy and my mother, Uta, to whom this book is dedicated.
Special thanks go to my friends Carolin, Alessandra, Paul, Anita, Luca, Jordan, Peter, Bernadette, Hans-Georg, Birgitta, Luciana, J. B., Maxine, Justus and Carl.

Long live life!

Translation from the German by John S. Southard
Editorial direction by Mirjam Ghisleni-Stemmle
Art direction by Hans-Georg Pospischil, Frankfurt (Main), Germany
Printed and bound by Kündig Druck AG, Baar, Switzerland

ISBN 3-908162-85-8